In His Hands

A Memorial to God's Faithfulness

In His Hands

A Memorial to God's Faithfulness

MADGE BECKON

GOSPEL FOLIO PRESS
P. O. Box 2041, Grand Rapids MI 49501-2041

Cover design by J. B. Nicholson, Jr.

Published by GOSPEL FOLIO PRESS
P. O. Box 2041, Grand Rapids, MI 49501-2041

ISBN 1-882701-27-5

PRINTED IN THE UNITED STATES OF AMERICA

DEDICATION

To the memory of Gifford

"The memory of the just is blessed."
<small>PROVERBS 10:7</small>

CONTENTS

THE DOUBLE CLASP

"And I give unto them eternal life; and they shall never perish,
neither shall any man pluck them out of My hand.
My Father, which gave them Me, is greater than all; and no man is
able to pluck them out of My Father's hand."
JOHN 10:28-29

The Saviour's hand—how close its hold,
That none can loosen, none can break.
No powers of heaven or earth or hell
That loving clasp can ever shake.

And over Jesus' wounded hand
The Father's hand of strength is laid,
Omnipotent to save and keep;
Thus is our surety surer made.

So, one beneath and one above,
Father and Son their hands unite.
How safe, how safe the ransomed are
Within the clasp of tender might!
ANNIE JOHNSON FLINT

From *Annie Johnson Flint's Best-Loved Poems*, Evangelical Publishers, Toronto

PREFACE

DEAR FRIEND,

I woke one morning recently with memories running through my mind—memories that reached back to the eve of my sixteenth birthday. It wasn't just another thought, for I again felt the fear that I had felt the night the Lord had answered a definite prayer for help. I lay there thinking about the details and the effect that experience had on my life. I realized anew how different things could have been, and most likely would have been, if God hadn't undertaken in such a precise way (see chapter 1 for the incident).

I put the incident out of my mind as I prepared for the day. Later, while reading Exodus 17, it came back to mind and I had the distinct feeling that God was trying to tell me something. Although there was no correlation in what I read with the experience that night, verse 14 caught my attention:

And the Lord said unto Moses, Write this for a memorial in a book.

I couldn't get past that verse as I thought of the various memorials in the Bible. It was as if God was telling me to retell this and other specific accounts of His protection, goodness, and provision as memorials and testimonies of His faithfulness.

From that original seed thought, "In His Hands: A Memorial to God's Faithfulness" came into existence. I have also included milestones, spiritual markers, and stepping

11

stones that bring to mind other times of decision, encouragement, and challenges in my life and in the lives of our family members. Others are experiences of encounters with God that I've witnessed in the lives of my dear Japanese friends who have profoundly touched us as I lived among them for 38 years.

The Lord has as many ways of deliverance as there are occasions to need them. I pass these accounts along to you, hoping that some of them might help you in times of crisis. May you, too, find the truth expressed in 1 Corinthians 10:13 a strong tower in your time of need:

There hath no temptation taken you but such as is common to man: but God is faithful, who will not suffer you to be tempted above that ye are able; but will with the temptation also make the way to escape, that ye may be able to bear it.

Yours because of Calvary,

MADGE BECKON
Englewood, Colorado

1
A MEMORIAL

"I remember the days of old; I meditate on all Thy works;
I muse on the work of Thy hands...Deliver me, O Lord, from mine
enemies: I flee unto Thee to hide me."
PSALM 143:5, 9

The year I turned sixteen was a memorable one. As is the case for most teenagers, it was a year of extreme emotional experiences. I was either on Cloud Nine or down in the pits, and I would change from one extreme to another in a matter of minutes. My mother was sick, we had no finances with which to hire help—and Mother certainly needed help! My baby brother, born in April, needed care. The rest of the family required attention as well, to say nothing of the washing, ironing, cooking, and cleaning. That summer I decided to drop out of school and manage the household until my mother was back on her feet.

Putting this decision into practice, however, is quite a story. Despite all the activities that came with fulfilling the duties of a minister's housekeeper, I found time to date. And it was through my dating that God got my attention.

I had been dating a young man seven years my senior. He was not exactly a spiritual help to me, and certainly was not of a caliber that matched the role I was called upon to fulfill. Although he was a professing Christian, he was more world-ly-wise than spiritual. But I was in love, or at least I felt I was, and that was all that mattered to me.

On the eve of my sixteenth birthday, we went on a double date. After we dropped off the other young man's date, he joined us in the front seat. It was getting late, so I told my friend that I should be getting home because my parents would be worried about me. From that moment on, I had an ominous feeling that trouble was brewing. Then I became aware that we were headed in the opposite direction from my house!

I mentioned that fact to my date, but it brought only laughter from both the young fellows. My date continued driving in the same direction, away from the road home. He deliberately ignored my request to be taken home. My heart skipped more than one beat when we turned off the main road onto a narrow lane. That route narrowed further as each half mile passed until it finally ended in an old farmyard. The car stopped in front of an abandoned house. I thought I knew the area, but now I didn't recognize anything; I had no idea where we were.

My date turned the ignition off. As I heard the engine die, my heart turned to stone and my bones chilled. Then the two young men broke out into diabolical laughter as if they were enjoying a dark secret together. I was overtaken by a desperate, helpless feeling of terror. I was the victim of a conspiracy and there was absolutely no one to help me.

Or was there? Up to that point, I had not prayed about my relationship with this young man. However, at that moment thoughts of God flooded my mind. I immediately bowed my head and cried out to Him from the depths of my soul. In a flash I realized that what my body and emotions had been desiring was not what I wanted after all.

Instantly I made a fresh commitment to the Lord. I sought His gracious forgiveness for my carelessness and wrong desires. I realized that I had completely failed to seek His wisdom and will for my life. I realized, too, that, more than physical safety, I wanted spiritual protection. I see now that the preaching of the cross which I had embraced when I was saved became in reality the power of God that night for both my physical and spiritual safety. Although I was not conscious of the truth, it was Christ living within me who protected my purity.

Miraculously, without either of the young men touching me, my date started the car, turned it around, and headed out of the driveway. Without saying a word, we drove to my home. I silently continued my prayer that I would never find myself in such circumstances again. I passed a milestone that night which I have never forgotten. I learned that God is a very present help in time of trouble (Ps. 46:1). It was only His graciousness that kept me from harm in answer to my desperate prayer.

That night, the lesson I learned about the Lord's sovereign purpose for me has kept me from similar danger many times since. The Lord's protection today still stands as a monument that is as real to me as the stone pillars or cairns the people raised in Old Testament times to memorialize God's dealing in their lives (see Gen. 28:18; 31:46; 35:14; Josh. 4:4-9). So I share this and similar experiences as reminders of God's faithfulness. He is still the very same refuge and present help in time of trouble that He was to Jacob, Joshua, the Israelites at Gilgal, and the many others who populate the pages of Scripture.

2
AN ACCEPTABLE SACRIFICE

"Verily I say unto you, Wheresoever this gospel shall be preached in the whole world, there shall also this, that this woman hath done, be told for a memorial of her."
MATTHEW 26:13

One of the greatest joys of my return visits to Japan is to hear the testimonies of Christians who have proved that the Lord's grace is sufficient. I listened to one such testimony while visiting in the home of one of my former Sunday school students. I had watched her consistent Christian life as demonstrated before her family and community, but I never knew what this had actually cost her. This dear sister stands out as a clear example of how God had His hand on one young life. Through Sunday school He had implanted in her heart the desire to know Him, and had kept her through times of great trial. Hearing her testimony alone was reward enough for all the hours I invested in children's work.

It was a bit deflating when she laughingly admitted that she couldn't recall anything I had taught her, but she did remember two things: learning Bible verses and swimming in our pool as a reward for attendance. Gifford had enlarged the original fish pond in the garden and made it into a pool six feet wide, eighteen feet long, and three feet deep. He had done it so our three daughters could learn to swim and cool off on hot summer days.

Our girls had exclusive rights to the pool during the week

and on Saturday mornings, but on Saturday afternoons they shared the pool with the Sunday school students who had attended for three consecutive Sundays. This student kept perfect attendance for this privilege. Such a reward wouldn't work today, because there are plenty of public pools, but then it was a big deal. Although this dear sister, who is now an elder's wife, had not been saved while attending Sunday school, the desire to know the One, True, Living God had been planted.

From the start, the girl's mother was not happy about her interest in Sunday school. When she entered junior high school, her mother openly opposed her coming. By the time she went to college, she seemed to have pretty much forgotten about God and we didn't see her for at least ten years.

The Lord had not forgotten her, however. He placed her as a teacher in a preschool where she met a believer, a bright, faithful witness for Christ. They soon struck up a friendship. Through her contact with this teacher, the seeds of truth she had heard years before in Sunday school were revived and began to grow. After a few months of working with her believing coworker, she accepted an invitation to attend camp during their summer break.

I don't have vivid memories of her Sunday school years, but I certainly remember the morning at camp when she saw the truth and accepted Christ as her Saviour. The friend who had invited her to camp came into the kitchen and told me that this young lady was alone in her room and very upset. It was recreational time and she should have been outdoors with the rest of the young people. Although she had urged her to go out, she had refused. Her friend added that she thought she really wanted to get saved.

I soon recruited a volunteer to take over my kitchen responsibilities and went to her. Deeply under the conviction of sin and fearing the certain penalty of sin, she was so receptive to the gospel. When she realized that her judgment had been paid for by Christ on the cross, she received Him joyfully as her Lord and Saviour. The joy of her salvation has been expressed in her very special smile ever since.

What I never knew until that morning of my return visit to Japan was the price this young believer paid soon after her decision to follow Christ. Her mother had adamantly opposed her attending anything that had to do with the "foreigner's religion." This was largely because she was convinced that no one of significant social standing would consider her daughter as a marriage partner for their son if she became known as a Christian. As a result of this fear, the mother forbade her daughter to attend any services while she lived at home.

The daughter immediately realized the difficulty of her choice. She would either have to comply with her mother's wishes or move out and live on her own. Living on her own was financially impossible for her at the time.

After hearing this news, she told her mother politely but firmly that she was going to the Christian camp, regardless of the result. She left the house in fear and trembling that first night, but hardly thought it would come to a head so quickly.

When she returned home, the front door was locked. It was cold and drizzling, but no amount of calling and knocking brought either her father or mother to the door. She had counted the cost before, but experiencing it was quite another matter. For two hours she sat on a large rock in their garden, huddled under her umbrella. Wondering what she should do, she pled with the Lord to reveal His will for her.

When she reached this part of her story, I stopped her and asked why she hadn't come to our house to spend the night. We would gladly have taken her in. Her answer surprised me and enabled me to understand why she had never shared this story before. If she was going to be a Christian in Japan, she explained, she needed to resolve the issue. It was her problem, not the foreigners. She needed to find out for herself if God was real or not. She had to prove Him for herself. And prove

Him she did. It was a struggle for her to pass this first milestone, but a struggle that served her well through life.

Shortly after midnight on that rainy night, the lock on the front door quietly turned and she heard a squeak as the door opened slightly. Even in the darkness she recognized the form of her father. They exchanged no words that night nor the following morning. According to Japanese culture, the father had the right to permit the girl to enter the home without going through the mother. The father was a peace-loving man and didn't want to battle his wife out in the open, so waited until the mother was asleep to unlock the door. The following morning, the mother was aware of his actions and didn't give in easily, but by not bringing about an outright confrontation, the father fought and won the battle in silence.

The daughter continued to live at home until her marriage, and throughout those difficult years never compromised her faith. She had the assurance that she had followed the leading of the Lord that night, and felt He would continue what He had started. She followed her mother's wishes wherever they did not conflict with Scripture, and won her heart through helpfulness and love. A few years later, in spite of her mother's fears, she married into a socially acceptable family.

Her husband taught in a school for handicapped children. Not too long after their marriage, they assumed the management of the Christian bookstore in Takasaki and moved into the apartment above the store. A short time later, her mother died. For a time her father lived alone, but when he was diagnosed with cancer, the couple offered to move back home to care for him, which was a relief to the other family members. She cared for her father ungrudgingly for a few years until his death. Under her loving care he listened to and received the gospel, but he was never a strong enough Christian to remove the family shrine from the home completely. He moved it into his room, but it was still there.

After the father's death, a new crisis faced them. It was not only the issue of the shrine, but of the house itself. In Japan, the child who moves into the homestead automatically takes over the ancestral rites, which means making daily offerings and presiding over family rituals on special memorial days. As Christians, they could not accept this responsibility. Although the problem was largely hers, she had the full support of her husband. They chose to give up all rights to the home, which was a financially painful step to take. By this time they had three young sons, so it was not easy to give up their property rights. They moved out nonetheless.

After one month passed, the other family members held a counsel. As a result of their consultation, one of the brothers called her and explained that the whole family appreciated her loving care of their father. Since the other siblings owned their homes, they had concluded that she and her family should move back in and assume ownership of the homestead. I don't know the details of the arrangement, but assume it was satisfactory to all concerned. The brother also agreed to take the family shrine into his home and carry on the rituals in their place.

Testing like this is fairly common in Japan. Believers there are forced early in their Christian faith to make clear commitments to stand for Christ. We can help them by prayer.

Because she stood for the Lord in these crises, this dear believer is now in a position to help other women who face similar circumstances. She and her husband use their home as a refuge for believers and unsaved alike. As I sat with them and a group of other Christians, I once again saw proof that those who lose their lives for Jesus Christ and His gospel's sake will save them in the end (Lk. 9:24). She is a good example that those who present themselves as living sacrifices, holy and acceptable by Christ Jesus, not only please God but in the end prove what that good, acceptable, and perfect will of the Lord is for them.

3
A Stroke of Bad Luck?

"Remember that thou magnify His work, which men behold.
Every man may see it; man may behold it afar off.
Behold, God is great…"
JOB 36:24-26

"How long did he say it would take to get the part?"

"About three hours," my husband, Gifford, answered.

I groaned as I thought of spending three hours simmering in the heat while waiting for our car to be repaired. This was a far cry from the plans we had when we set off from the house. As new missionaries in Japan, we had great hopes for an outreach with the gospel. We were on our way to a planned weekly meeting in a new area—all set with Gospels of John, tracts, accordion, and song sheets, but the car broke down halfway there. Fortunately, it happened in a convenient place where we could push it downhill to a garage.

I would have enjoyed a stroll beside the cool stream nearby, but for Gifford this gave opportunity for a new adventure in a town where we'd never had a street meeting. He was excited, and not willing to forfeit the chance. To my way of thinking, it was a stroke of bad luck to be endured. Judging from experience, I had my doubts about being on our way in the three hours the man at the garage had promised. However, the fact that we would not be at our scheduled meeting didn't even seem to daunt Gifford's spirit. He was sure that the gospel had never been preached in that town before, so he saw every person we met as a potential prospect for salvation. Watching him, I did catch a bit of his enthusiasm, so tried to keep step. At least, I didn't want to hold him back.

Leaving the garage, we walked for at least thirty minutes before we found a spot in the street that was wide enough to set up the song sheet poster frame and still allow people to walk around it. In those days in Japan, a tall American and his wife, playing an accordion and singing gospel songs in Japanese, never failed to attract a gathering of onlookers. The problem was not in getting a crowd, but in the fact that the police would soon appear if the crowd became too large and started to interfere with the town's daily business. We didn't want to upset anyone.

As usual, it took only a minute for people to begin gathering. They were eager to hear what this foreigner had to say to them in their own language. We were still in language school, so our unpolished Japanese left much to be desired in the way of proper grammar, but the Japanese are a patient and understanding people. The simple fact that they gathered around us was incentive enough to begin.

Gifford was never happier than when he was preaching the gospel, and it showed. Whenever the crowd got restless, he'd stop speaking, sing another song, and then he was fresh and ready to begin again. By that time, the crowd had changed, some leaving and others wandering back. This went on for well over two hours. Between each message we passed out tracts and Gospels of John. Literally hundreds of people heard the gospel message and most of them took the literature offered.

At the end of our time, we were very hot and weary, but extremely happy. We gathered up our things and walked back to the garage. I don't believe we had to wait for our car, but I can't remember the details.

As far as we could tell, there was no response of a permanent nature to our meeting. We had no idea how God was using the experience for good.

24

About six months later, however, a student in a school uni-
form appeared at our front door. He carried a wrapped gift in
his hand. Our first assumption was that the gift was to prepare
our hearts to teach him English or to honor some other
request. We were pleasantly surprised when he accepted our
invitation to come in, and told us the reason for his errand.

His older sister, who was a very sick young lady, had been
lying on her mat directly behind the open window in front of
which we had held our street meeting the day our car broke
down. She had listened to us the whole time. She was deeply
touched by the message of God's love, His hatred for sin, and
the provision He had made through the death of His own Son.
She was impressed by God's love for the Japanese by sending
Jesus Christ, and then for Him to send someone to her own
home to tell her about it. Had she chosen to do so, she could
have pulled the curtain aside and reached for a tract herself,
but the reticent Japanese culture didn't permit that, so she
asked her brother to go out the back door and ask for the literature. She later read and reread all the literature we had
offered. All she saw confirmed the messages she had heard.

Her brother had come to ask us if we would visit his sister
because she wanted the eternal life that was available through
Jesus Christ. She had read the Gospel of John and wanted to
hear more. He had found our house from the address stamped
on the back of each piece. She couldn't fully understand what
she had read, but what she did understand she trusted to be
true because it spoke to her heart.

To show her appreciation, she had hand-sewn a lovely
Japanese doll and had sent her brother to deliver it to us. We
were grateful for her gift, but far more appreciative of the
wonderful news we had just heard. Although her brother was
not particularly interested in the Bible, he was polite and out
of love for his sister had found us. He stayed for a cup of tea.

Japanese culture requires a return gift, and we were hard
pressed to find something appropriate in the house until we

remembered our new copy of the *Daily Light* that we had just bought. The *Daily Light* is an all-Scripture devotional book for believers and was hardly appropriate for a seeker, but it was all we had. We sent it back with him with our love and prayers, and agreed to visit his sister at the next convenient time. As a result of this contact, we visited her often and a life-long friendship was formed.

Some time later, the brother again appeared at our front door. This time he was interested in the gospel. As a result of his second visit, we began stopping to see them on our way to the city of Takasaki where we had weekly meetings. It was on one of these visits that he decided to ride with us to the service. It wasn't long before this became a weekly occurrence.

That fall, he moved to Tokyo to attend university. Since he had not as yet professed salvation, we were concerned about losing this weekly contact with him. Unknown to us, he borrowed his sister's *Daily Light* and began reading it. It wasn't too much later when he came for a visit, that he told us he also had believed in Jesus Christ as his personal Saviour.

The brother's testimony was as amazing as his sister's. He was saved through reading the *Daily Light* alone in his room in Tokyo. While reading it, the simplicity of Christ's substitutionary death on the cross became a living reality to him. We were amazed that God had used the book we had sent as a gift to the sister, not because we felt it was appropriate for an unsaved person, but because it had been the only thing new we had in the house to give at the time of the brother's first visit. It had indeed been light upon his dark path.

The brother's spiritual progress was unusual and we were pleased to see his steady growth. Soon after his baptism, however, we left for a furlough in the United States. This furlough became an extended one due to medical problems that involved surgery for both of us. Although we lost personal contact with the brother at the time, the Lord is constantly at work, performing the work He has begun. While the young man was at the university in Tokyo, he attended an evangelical church where the Lord burdened his heart about preaching the gospel. Today he ministers in a Japanese congregation in Los Angeles. It reminds me of Philippians 1:6, which states that we can be "...confident of this very thing, that He who has begun a good work in you will perform it until the day of Jesus Christ" (Phil. 1:6).

Without doubt, the gospel of Christ is the power of God unto salvation. Whether it is delivered from the lips of a missionary who still struggles with the language, or from the pages of a book written for believers, the Lord can open blind eyes to the truth and draw needy sinners to Himself. Memories of such ongoing stories serve to remind us that there is no such thing as a stroke of bad luck when God is involved. I would urge you to pray faithfully that God will continue to use this dear middle-aged brother in Christ who stands as a monument to God's overruling purposes.

4
BULLIES

"When my soul fainted within me I remembered the Lord: and my prayer came in unto Thee, into Thine holy temple."
JONAH 2:7

One day my memory file suddenly spilled out a frightening experience I had when I was about seven or eight years old. The memory came to mind quite unbidden. A friend (who was about my age) and I had gone for a walk one morning, looking for something exciting to do. Suddenly we heard two of the town's biggest bullies following us. We glanced back at them, and our thoughts of looking for fun vanished quickly. The boys were about our own age but twice our size, and we knew they had no good intentions. When we picked up speed, so did they.

Our hearts beat in time as we walked faster. The situation grew worse because the boys were coming closer by the minute. They began shouting out threats of what they were going to do to us. Even though we were in a residential area, there was not another soul in sight.

The boys finally caught up with us. My friend and I froze with fear and then burst into tears. This only encouraged and pleased our tormentors. They began blocking our way until we were just two very frightened little girls standing in the middle of the sidewalk screaming our heads off. Whether the boys would actually have carried out their threats remains a mystery, but believe me, in our imaginations it was real enough. At that moment I had no thought of calling to God in prayer, but He was there anyway.

Suddenly my eye caught movement behind the screen door of a nearby porch. Through the door I saw the form of a man, a *big* man. I broke into a run, and dashed onto his porch where I begged him to help us get past those terrible boys. In a second he assessed the situation, and came out of the house. One glance at his huge frame and the bullies disappeared.

I stammered our plight to the man and pleaded with him to walk back up the hill with us. He said he was busy and couldn't do that. As hard as we tried, we couldn't get him to change his mind. However, he offered to stand watch until we were up the hill. With that he walked to the sidewalk and rested his big foot on a fence post. We were told to start off.

Thankfully, he was a man of his word. Every time we turned back to see if he was still standing there, he waved us on. We tried to run, but were constantly slowed down by our backward glances.

His huge form is still clear in my mind. I can see him resting his foot on the fence post, his chin in his hand, no doubt wishing we would hurry. Needless to say, the bullies did not show up again. They had met their match. As we turned the corner, the man walked slowly back into his yard. With one final wave, we broke into a run and raced all the way home.

As I think back to those frightening moments, I'm grateful for the great comfort we found in the presence of one man who was a perfect stranger. Although he wouldn't go with us, he did stand watch until we were out of danger.

When I was debating whether to go back to Japan alone after Gifford's death, the Lord used Exodus 33:14 to assure me that He wouldn't just stand there with His foot on the fence post. He would never turn His back on me and walk back into His yard.

I had always gone to Japan with a husband who took care of all the logistics. Then the Lord assured me: *"My presence shall go with thee, and I will give thee rest"* (Ex. 33:14). I still wrestled with the idea that I felt much more secure with a flesh and blood companion, but my Lord soon assured me that He would be enough.

He, the very Lord of the universe, promised me personally that He would go with me. Countless were the times, especially during the first few years of living alone, when the Lord used the image of the stranger to bring me back to this promise. The promise of His presence in my life has enabled me to drop off to sleep many times when I otherwise would have lain awake in fear, listening to the creaks of my house or dreading a disturbing late-night telephone call. At one period there was one strange man who would, about two o'clock in the morning, assure me over the phone in a slurred, drunken voice that he loved me—almost as frightening as little girls being chased by bullies!

At times like that, another verse the Lord often used as a monument of strength was Hebrews 13:5-6—

> *"...He hath said, I will never leave thee, nor forsake thee. So that we may boldly say, The Lord is my helper, and I will not fear what man shall do unto me."*

The gap between my almighty Lord and mere man is far, far greater than the difference between the size and strength of a full-grown man and schoolboys. God, the same God who delivered His people from the inhabitants of the Promised Land, is the same One who makes His promise to be with us at all times and in all circumstances. It is good to periodically erect monuments to remind ourselves that Jesus Christ is the same today as He was in the yesteryears, and He always will be.

5
CATARACT SURGERY

"Remembering mine affliction and my misery, the wormwood and the gall. My soul hath them still in remembrance..."
LAMENTATIONS 3:19-20

I was devastated by the news that my dear grandfather had fallen out of bed the night following cataract surgery and had ripped out his stitches. I was even more devastated when the doctor confirmed that he was totally blind. Grandpa would never see me again. This was bad news for a young child. I hardly understood what cataracts were, but it seemed very serious to me if the operation caused blindness.

Things went from bad to worse for Grandpa. He couldn't cope with the adjustment to blindness. It was a great hardship for him, and for Grandma, too. He was a very independent man and wanted to continue his work in the barn; he insisted on going out there. At times Grandma would find him in the weirdest places where he had fallen. Only the Lord protected him from being seriously hurt. I wanted so badly to help him and would go with him to the barn, but I only got in the way. It was sad to watch him grope around and often injure himself. How my heart ached for him, but there was absolutely nothing I could do to make him see again.

Now I'm of the age to have cataracts. When one has cataracts, a film clouds the lens of the eye, causing it to become opaque and impervious to light. Only a surgeon can remove the cataract and enable the eye to operate normally again. I know that at some time in the future surgery will be inevitable for me. I don't fear the operation now as I did years ago. I know that if I'm ever to recover my good vision, the operation must be done. A skilled surgeon must cut away the cataracts so that I will see clearly.

This morning I had a phone conversation with my youngest daughter that reminded me about cataracts—not visual cataracts, but spiritual cataracts. She said, " Oh, Mother, if we could only make her see, but we can't. Only the Holy Spirit can open her eyes to the truth." She was not talking about physical eyes, but spiritual eyes that had clouded over. The Bible describes this malady as having a veil over one's eyes. Both veils and cataracts keep us from seeing clearly. Both make us impervious to God's light. Both require the surgeon's touch if we are to see clearly again.

My daughter's comment about leaving this surgery to the Lord set my mind to working. I can recall many times when I've tried to scalpel a cataract off someone's eyes, yet only one Surgeon qualifies to do this delicate operation. We can help Him in various ways, perhaps, but only the touch of the Lord's hand can do the job successfully. Only the One who created the eye has the healing touch to peel off the obstructing film. Thankfully He does it graciously and successfully.

Yet we so often grope about for years before we are willing to entrust ourselves to the Surgeon's hands. It is so pitiful to watch a believer endure poor spiritual vision, especially when it is someone we love. But my daughter's comment brought peace to my heart as we covenanted together to pray for the person we were concerned about and to leave the operation in His loving hands. He does ask us to help Him, though, through prayer, and this we are happy to do.

The story of the two disciples on the road to Emmaus (see Lk. 24) has helped me realize how the Lord performs this delicate surgery. When the Lord joined the two on the road heading northwest out of Jerusalem, He knew they were suffering an acute case of spiritual cataracts. Their disappointment in recent events, involving their precious and respected Leader, had blinded their eyes to the truth of God's plan for salvation. They had built their hopes on Christ's setting up His kingdom on earth at that time, but He had been murdered on a cross. Instead of reigning, He had died in agony. They reasoned that no good could come from His death. One glance at their sad faces and flagging energy revealed their spiritual state.

He corrected their lack of vision by performing an operation right there as they walked. He simply lifted the scales from their eyes. He did so by bringing them back to the Scriptures and giving them a review of God's overall plan for salvation. Through the Old Testament, He showed them God's marvelous plan, and that the recent happenings in Jerusalem were an essential part of that plan from before the beginning of time. When He removed the cataracts from these dear disciples' eyes, and they could see God's light again, the transformation was thrilling. They had joy. They had energy enough to continue the journey that had begun so dejectedly a short time before.

Since the creation of the world, our Saviour and Surgeon has specialized in removing cataracts from spiritual eyes. We have no cure for ourselves nor for others, but we can help by coming to Him for surgery and then by bringing others. I believe the sight of His scarred, nail-pierced hands brought about the final removal of the veil. As they caught a glimpse of those blessed hands when He broke the bread before them, the disciples once more had perfect sight. They saw at that instant that He was indeed the Messiah, sent by the Father to redeem them from their sins. No doubt, Isaiah 53 flooded their hearts, and their spiritual vision was fully restored.

"Give me a sight, O Saviour, of Thy wondrous love to me;
Of the love that brought Thee down to earth to die on Calvary."

6
CHOSEN TO APPROACH

"Our fathers understood not Thy wonders in Egypt; they remembered not the multitude of Thy mercies; but provoked Him at the sea, even at the Red sea. Nevertheless He saved them for His name's sake, that He might make His mighty power to be known."
PSALM 106:7-8

What do you do when a portion of Scripture seems to be in direct opposition to what you are feeling at a given time? I faced such a quandary one morning when I got the news that a proposal for an arranged marriage had been refused.

Let me explain the situation. In Japan, marriages generally are arranged by the family, which requires the help of a middleman. In cases where a believer refuses to marry an unsaved person who has been chosen, a respected and seasoned Christian serves in the capacity of choosing a suitable partner.

We were visiting in the home of a Christian who was responsible for doing this for a young sister. After he had broken the news that the young man's family was not pleased with the girl's family and had refused to talk further, we read the Bible together. The man opened to James 5. As he came to the eleventh verse and we read it together, I was ambushed by a nagging doubt about the Lord's pity and tender mercy.

Behold, we count them happy which endure. Ye have heard of the patience of Job, and have seen the end of the Lord; that the Lord is very pitiful and of tender mercy.

I realized at the time that we had not yet seen the end which the Lord had planned, but it did not appear to me that God was either pitiful or of tender mercy. My dear friend had been hurt again, and I was hurting with her. Was I expected to count her happy? She had endured this same experience twice before. Yet James said that the Lord took pity and that He was tender and gracious. I had trouble bringing these thoughts into submission to Christ.

I didn't know whether it was best to share the struggle I was feeling or not. I didn't know if I should let them know honestly that missionaries also have times when they doubt that things truly are as they are written in the Bible.

A summary of the circumstances that led up to this situation may help you understand why I was so disappointed with the news. Unfortunate circumstances in the girl's home had prompted the elders in the assembly to step in and help our sister find a suitable mate to marry. The Christian young lady was a lovely person. She had a personable disposition and was very attractive, but she also had an older sister with a long history of emotional disorders. So whenever her resumé was submitted to a family considering marriage for their son, they turned her down for this reason. Everything was in her favor except for this family problem, for which she was not responsible.

After this young woman was refused a second time, we felt we had the perfect family for the young lady. They were believers and we were sure they would not give in to this prejudice, but alas, that was not so. The mother was adamant that her son was not going to bring emotional sickness into their family, and that was the end of the conversation! I knew that the young man himself was more than willing to take the risk because he was pleased with the young woman's qualities in every way, but his family would not hear of it. That is what broke my heart because I had imagined them as a lovely couple who would begin a fine Christian home. It was not to be.

When the same situation was repeated, I felt great sympathy for my sister in the Lord.

After our reading, when the elder and his wife prayed about the matter, I fought my own private battle with the Lord over the issue. I'd previously had trouble with the book of Job, and this situation didn't help my feelings. But the Lord graciously stepped in and brought to my mind the two little words, "the end." He seemed to say to me, "Madge, have patience. You can't see the end, but I can." He seemed to be telling me to let Him handle things. In the matter of arranging marriages, I had always enjoyed helping Him. It was a great joy, but He didn't need nor want my interference this time. He made it very clear to me that I was to keep out and believe that He *was* pitiful, tender hearted, and that He *would* show His mercy later. I was not to take up the cause of this young lady against Him, nor was I to express my feelings to anyone, for she was not a victim in His eyes. Rather, He had chosen her to lean on Him. She was caused, by circumstances, to approach Him in prayer. As described in Psalms 65:4, she was chosen to approach Him in a special way.

> Blessed is the [wo]man whom Thou choosest, and causeth to approach unto Thee, that [s]he may dwell in thy courts: we shall be satisfied with the goodness of Thy house....

After a few tears together, and much more prayer, I was able to turn it over to the Lord. This dear sister and I became very close friends, and the Lord gave us a ministry together, working with other single women. But it wasn't too long before the Lord sent a young man into her life who saw her for who she really was; he approached the elders and asked for her hand in marriage. He had to stand up against family opposition, but he won her hand in marriage. God richly blessed their life together.

It wasn't until I sat in her living room during my trip back to Japan in 1995, when all these memories came to mind, that

I realized just how blessed and happy she really was. At the dining room table, I sat directly across from her beautiful twenty-year-old daughter and next to her warm-hearted, loving husband. The atmosphere was both happy and peaceful. I could feel the presence of God.

As I glanced at all the people seated in this couple's home— believers and unsaved alike—I had another private conversation with my Lord. I thanked Him that He had given me the assurance that heartbreaking morning so many years ago, that He was working all the details out for good. There before me was proof that He truly had the best plan for her life. He had been pitiful, and certainly proved to be of tender mercies. I fought the tears of joy which threatened to spill over in gratitude.

Admittedly, it had taken time, but during that time, she, like Job, had approached God. She learned to fellowship with Him, and God had made Himself real to her. She had matured into a contented Christian, and her home had been used by God to add many to the church of Christ through weekly cottage meetings.

I observed this godly woman's face as she extended Christian hospitality, and I knew that she had found the joy of service for the Lord. Her beaming face revealed that she was definitely one of those about whom the Scripture says, "For whosoever would save his life shall lose it; but whosoever shall lose his life for My sake and the gospel's, the same shall save it" (Mk. 8:35).

She had accepted the disappointment of rejection and was willing to stay single if the Lord wished it so. She did not let it hinder her in her zeal for the Lord. What I witnessed that night revealed that she had found a satisfying life because God had chosen her to approach Him.

7
CLOSE ENOUGH TO CATCH IT

"The desire of our soul is to Thy name, and to the remembrance of Thee. With my soul have I desired Thee in the night; yea, with my spirit within me will I seek Thee early..."
ISAIAH 26:8-9

One day, not too long after my husband passed away, one of my daughters and I walked down a busy street in Los Angeles. A well-dressed young man approached us from the opposite direction. He was evidently quite preoccupied because he nearly walked into us before he noticed us. At the last moment, he politely stepped aside and avoided a collision. But we were close enough that I got a good whiff of his after shave lotion, which I immediately recognized as the same scent my late husband had used. The sudden nostalgia produced by the fragrance caused such an emotional sensation that I had a physical reaction of nausea and feelings of deep longings for Gifford. When one looses someone they dearly love, everything about that person becomes precious, even the aroma of their shaving lotion.

Although this incident happened a number of years ago, it came to mind this morning when I read Psalm 45:6-8.

Thy throne, O God, is for ever and ever: the scepter of Thy kingdom is a right scepter. Thou lovest righteousness, and hatest wickedness: therefore God, Thy God, hath anointed Thee with the oil of gladness above Thy fellows. All Thy garments smell of

41

myrrh, and aloes, and cassia, out of the ivory palaces, whereby they have made Thee glad.

These verses brought back my memories of shaving lotion and led me to think about the woman in Luke 7:36-50 who anointed Christ. She had such a close relationship with, and appreciation of, Christ that I envied her. I wondered how she developed such a relationship. How did she understand that His death was imminent and that it was for her personally? I coveted her spirit of worship as I saw her so taken up with these thoughts of love that nothing mattered but her desire to make Him happy. No price was too great to express her love for Him before He died. Somehow the lingering thoughts of the shaving lotion incident and the sweet savor of Christ in this woman's life gave me an overwhelming desire to know Him and love Him in as real a sense as I did Gifford.

I read the passage again and the Lord showed me why she perceived His worth and worship to this extent. This discovery gave me hope that some day I would be able to do the same. The Lord reminded Simon that He had given the Lord no kiss, but she had constantly kissed His feet. A kiss is a token of love expressed. Though she may have known little of what lay ahead for those feet, soon to be spiked to a cross, her closeness to Him seems to have given her a hint of the sweet aroma of heaven which He bore about His person.

Did she have a similar feeling to the one Isaac must have had when he stood back and watched the ram die for him? Where he had lain moments before, Isaac saw himself on that altar, in that ram offered as a sweet savor burnt offering. What joy in the life and freedom he now possessed!

So did the woman Luke mentions; she worshipped in the true sense of the word. The Lord linked the kissing of His feet and the anointing of His head with her longing for the forgiveness of sins. The kissing, the anointing, and the tears of gratitude, were all expressions of her appreciation of how much she had been forgiven. We learn to think of sin in the way He evaluates it by being close to Him. This was Simon's (and sometimes our) problem: it was not that he needed to be forgiven only a little, but that he little understood how much he owed to that Man at his table.

In Old Testament days, incense was to be kept solely for God. I now see that God wants me to be pleased with the fragrance of the incense of Christ's garments. This means I have to be in close enough proximity to Him to recognize and enjoy His aroma. I am left with a great longing to feel Christ as near and dear as the woman in Luke 7. Much of the special joy in worship is in catching the lingering fragrance of His love and delighting in the sweetness of His forgiveness.

8
CONTENTED

"The righteous shall be in everlasting remembrance."
PSALM 112:6

It was a very happy day when the Israelites went in to claim the Promised Land. That tremendous milestone was never to be forgotten. But surely it should be no happier for them than it is for any believer today who enters into the "rest" which the author of Hebrews (chs. 3 & 4) describes. I know there are various definitions for "rest" but to me, there is no better name for it than contentment.

Contentment is like a purring cat. I enjoy a cat climbing into my lap, settling down, and beginning to purr. That cat is at rest. It is content where it is, with what it has, and is at peace with the world in the safety and warmth of its owner's lap.

Paul told Timothy in his first letter to him: "Godliness with contentment is great gain"(6:6). Contentment is a state of mind. It is not absorbed from those around us; it arises from within. If contentment were gained simply by the example of others, I would be a perfectly contented woman because my mother was about as perfect an example to me of contentment as I could ever have had. Unfortunately I've not been able to absorb perfect peace of mind from watching her. I remember a friend of mine looking up at Mom one day and saying, "Madge, your mother always looks so peaceful." I know that one's perception of a peaceful countenance can be a matter of comparison, but a peaceful look exemplified my mother.

My mother was a preacher's wife. She lived with criticism you wouldn't believe. Mom and I often cried together over the way people criticized her for not being more outgoing, or more like a typical minister's wife.

One example of the trials my mother endured occurred when I was in the sixth grade. I had a Sunday school teacher who had a "crush" on my father and unashamedly said that she could be a better minister's wife than my mother. I knew she gave Mom a bad time, but I didn't know many of the details until fifty years later.

One day I drove through my old hometown and the Lord suddenly put it on my heart to visit my former teacher if she was still alive. After making inquiries, I found her in a nursing home. The welcome I received from her was unusually warm. She told me she was so glad to see me. The truth was she wanted to rid herself of a very guilty conscience. She had been convicted all these years, but couldn't bring herself to make things right. Oh, the sweetness and contentment that came following the clearing of her conscience. We had a great time of fellowship and prayer. Our time together explained much of what had happened. As I was leaving, she told me through tears how gracious my mother had been and what a wonderful woman she was.

Through Christ's work on the cross, the forgiveness had been available all those years, but the contentment had not. Sin had marred fellowship with God and it had constantly bothered her. The marvelous truth of God's perfect forgiveness penetrated her heart as she believed that God not only forgave her, but that Mother had also forgiven her long years before. Mother's trust in the Lord to work all things out for our family's good had enabled her to do so. God honored that faith even though it had taken fifty-some years to reach fruition. I was so glad the Lord had chosen me to relate this news to my mother. The teacher went to be with the Lord not too long after that experience. In my imagination I could see the open-arm-reception she gave Mom into heaven when she passed away a few years later.

Unfortunately, I did not learn contentment for myself through Mother's example. After I left home to establish my own family, my mother's peaceful contentment faded from view as I grew older. Now in later years, I'm having to develop contentment through my own relationship with the Lord. Personal contentment is obtained in solitude because it does not concern outside sources. It only grows within through implicit trust in the truth that God lives and richly rewards those who seek His companionship with all their hearts.

Scripture tells us that the real basis for contentment is to know God:

> *Acquaint now thyself with Him, and be at peace; thereby good shall come unto thee (Job 22:21).*

It's not easy to trust someone you don't know. As mentioned, the hindrance to God's rest, or contentment, is unbelief. Unbelief was the only thing that kept the Israelites out of the Promised Land, and it is the only thing that keeps me wandering about in my wilderness. I have to constantly pull myself up short when I become aware that my shoulders are stiff, my mind is whirling, and I feel restless within. I have to stop to ask myself the question, "Why?" Without fail, I find only one answer—unbelief.

Also, in Proverbs 9:10 we read:

> *The fear of the Lord is the beginning of wisdom, and the knowledge of the Holy One is understanding.*

As we come to know Christ as the Holy One, the perfect One who can do no wrong, we understand the "whys" of so many things. But even when we don't understand what is happening in our lives, by believing what He says about Himself, we become content, knowing He is able to handle any situation. Knowing that the Lord Jesus is a Man of His

Word, we should be able to commit our problems to Him and await His time for solution. As we trust His judgment, we will be able to accept His will, knowing He is always looking out for our good because He is the Friend above all friends. When we limit God, we are just as guilty as His people were in turning back to the wilderness, and the results will also be devastating (Ps. 78:41). In the meantime, we can face injustice, unfairness, rudeness, misunderstanding, criticism and the like, resting content by faith.

On the other hand, when we have been guilty of any of these things and have made them right, we can be assured of perfect forgiveness because He is faithful and just to forgive us. This truth is also received by faith.

If I really know God well enough to believe He is holy and right, I won't have trouble obeying His commands, either. I should find, as John did, that His commands are not grievous. Being content with this knowledge should make me able to obey without grumbling, resisting, or rebelling. He is utilizing these circumstances to develop my character and produce Christ-likeness in me. If I'm still disturbed because I don't understand all the "how-to's" of my life, there is no rest.

It was a devastating moment for Isaiah (6:1-8) when he had to acknowledge that he was a sinful man. It is equally so for me when I see that I don't deserve to live in His presence—in the land of rest, peace, and contentment—either. However, as in Isaiah's case, the moment of cleansing by the touch from the altar can be as glorious as confession is humbling.

9
COMFORT IN THE DARK

"Truly the light is sweet, and a pleasant thing it is for the eyes to behold the sun: but if a man live many years, and rejoice in them all; yet let him remember the days of darkness."
ECCLESIASTES 11:7-8

The words of our Lord Jesus Christ, "What I tell you in darkness, that speak ye in light" (Mt. 10:27) came to me tonight. I felt compelled to obey the admonition before the memory faded of an incident which happened within the first year of our missionary life in Japan.

Some very close missionary friends had been going through an extremely difficult time in the Lord's work. They shared little with us, but we knew what was going on through others. One day, I asked the wife how she was able to keep such a positive outlook on life, teach her Bible classes with the same sweet spirit we noticed when we first met her, and go on as if nothing out of the ordinary was happening. She then shared with me a Bible portion that they had received from the Lord as they faced their situation.

Their scripture was Psalm 66:10-12:

For Thou, O God, hast proved us: Thou hast tried us, as silver is tried. Thou broughtest us into the net: Thou laidst affliction upon our loins. Thou hast caused men to ride over our heads; we went through fire and through water: but Thou broughtest us out into a wealthy place.

She then explained how the hope of being brought out into a spiritually wealthy place had enabled them to carry on in the Lord's work with a quiet heart. At the time, the truth of those verses didn't mean all that much to me, but it was filed away in my mind. It was her absolute belief and trust in God that impressed me. I was amazed at their forgiving spirit.

About fourteen years later, Gifford and I experienced a time of darkness ourselves in the Lord's work, when the Lord brought this passage of Scripture to our minds. In the meantime, we had never made the correlation of the truly spiritually wealthy place God had brought this dear couple into and these verses. It was when we entered our dark time that God illuminated these verses for just such a time as we faced. We received great encouragement as we read them together.

I hesitate to reveal details of difficult situations, so suffice it to say that it was an extremely discouraging time. The work of ten years was lying at our feet in shambles. We faced exactly the same circumstances as our missionary friends had experienced: people were riding over our heads. It always hurts to have wheels run over your head, but even worse were the misunderstandings that followed.

Many were the fiery darts that hit their target. We were tempted to return to the United States and might have left the field had we had the means to do so. Especially as months passed, and it seemed that God would never work on our behalf were we tempted to quit our missionary career. But at each thought of despair, God brought to mind this passage and it began to work in our hearts. It created in us the desire to be brought out into a spiritually wealthy place and, like our friends before us, we also began to find Christ to be sufficient. He brought peace and quietness of heart through the same promise that He had given to our friends.

How much we needed that promise! As we hung onto it, we were able to carry on in the Lord's work. I hope that I can comfort someone today who needs this message as much as we were comforted through it when we desperately needed heaven's light to break into our darkness. May you be comforted through this, just as Christ comforted our hearts through the experience of our friends.

It is impossible to put on paper the many lessons God taught us while we were kept in the dark, but perhaps the most important one was the longing and need to know God in a more personal way. Our search brought us much closer together as a couple as we sought for this together.

Perhaps the second lesson was the need to teach young believers the importance of knowing how, in the work of the Lord, to build on a strong foundation:

...That thou mayest know how thou oughtest to behave thyself in the house of God, which is the church of the living God, the pillar and ground of the truth (1 Tim. 3:15).

And the things that thou hast heard of me among many witnesses, the same commit thou to faithful men, who shall be able to teach others also (2 Tim. 2:2).

It helped greatly, during the period of darkness, to remember that we were in the situation because God had allowed it. It was He who tested us, tried us, brought us into the net, and laid affliction on us. Therefore, it was God who would preserve us in it, and in His good time bring us out into the wealthy place spiritually. Happy is the man who knows that God is his guide unto death (see Ps. 48:14).

As for the wealthy place God brought us into, it was the supreme joy of seeing the Lord build character, strengthening and refining believers for His service. There is no joy like that of seeing spiritual children walking in the truth. We truly saw God *"...do exceeding abundantly above all that we ask or think, according to the power that worketh in us. Unto Him be glory in the church by Christ Jesus throughout all ages, world without end. Amen"* (Eph. 3:20-21).

51

10
DEFINITE PRAYERS, DEFINITE ANSWERS

"Bless the Lord, O my soul, and forget not all His benefits"
PSALM 103:2

Oh, for the faith of a child! When children want God to act on their behalf, they don't worry about theology, grammar, or even if their desire is the will of the Father in heaven. They simply feel a need and ask. At the breakfast table one morning, one of our three little girls opened her heart up to God and in all sincerity begged, "Lord, please send us some jam or peanut butter. I'm tired of eating plain toast."

I was shocked by her frankness to the Lord. At the same time, I had to suppress a laugh because it struck me as humorous that she would take it on herself to ask such a favor. I hadn't thought of it, nor had I dared to make such a direct request.

The Lord must have considered it to be a worthy and legitimate request, however, for it was only a matter of hours before an American G.I. arrived at our front door. He carried two large bags of groceries that he had purchased at the Commissary in Tokyo to give to us. Not only did the Lord send our daughter her jam and peanut butter, He sent many other goodies as well. We entertained our most welcomed guest in royal style. Our girls were thrilled beyond words. So was their mom!

I hesitate to share this next story, which is about finances too, because I fear that some readers will conclude that missionary life is all poverty. That is far from the truth—but we did have our times! As I record this incident, I pray that it will encourage you to pray for your own needs and to intercede for others, believing God provides, protects, heals, and strengthens in direct response to our definite prayers.

Not too long after our daughter's prayer for jam and peanut butter, we went through another hard time financially. I was concerned about the lack of protein in our diet, so I prayed a prayer similar to that of our daughter's. Did her example give me the courage to follow suit? At any rate, I prayed that the Lord would make it possible to add some form of protein to our diet that day; I felt we needed it.

My answer came through an elderly lady who had become a believer through our visits at the local hospital. After her release, she came to our home to express her thanks for our ministry while she had been hospitalized. A common Japanese custom, it is never expressed without a gift.

Clutching a cloth bag and with effusive apologies as she pulled out its contents, she asked, "Do you know what this stuff is? It smells like it is rotten." I knew at once what it was—cheese! This country woman had never included cheese in her diet. When looking for a suitable gift to take to us, her daughter had told her that foreigners ate cheese, assuring her it was not spoiled, and suggested that it would make a good gift to us.

In those days in Japan, cheese was an extremely expensive item. Someone had given it to the woman as a gift and she passed it on to us. Little did she know that she had been sent on a special mission for the Lord that very day. Without doubt, the cheese was beneficial to us, but I think her gift at that time was far more beneficial to my faith. On another occasion, the Lord sent fruit when we were craving it. It was a gift of gratitude for Gifford's judging an English contest.

The longer I sit here, the further my mind reaches back into the past. Let me share only one more incident that comes to mind. Upon receiving orders from the American Embassy to leave China because of Communist activities, we headed for Japan. But in Hong Kong we were informed that we couldn't take our baby into Japan because the sanitation conditions were still so bad in the aftermath of the war. They said we would have to wait until the baby was a year old, so we moved to Taiwan to wait there.

By Esther's first birthday, we were well established and happy in the work of the Lord in Taiwan. That all came to an abrupt end when another letter came from the United States Embassy stating that Taiwan was facing a crisis with China. All the married people with children were advised to leave. We were given three days in which to dispose of our goods, get our visas, and purchase tickets to Japan. The combination of the unexpected delay, the cost of tickets, having to set up housekeeping yet again, and the need to hire a tutor to teach us Japanese, had depleted our resources. Furthermore, our correspondence had not caught up with us because our friends didn't know about our sudden move.

We scraped along for a while, but we steadily got behind in our finances. I'm so thankful that Paul was very frank in his correspondence. For example, 2 Corinthians 6:4-10 states:

But in all things commending ourselves as the ministers of God, in much patience, in afflictions, in necessities, in distresses....

Paul was frank in admitting that everything didn't work out smoothly for him at times, either. Without Paul's forthrightness, we might have assumed that we were out of the will of the Lord, and had not been led by the Lord to go to Japan. A new culture, lack of finances, and other hardships were quite a contrast to the joy we had been experiencing in Taiwan, so it would have been easy to come to that conclusion. We managed somehow to keep body and soul together, but our financial situation daily became more desperate.

During this difficult period, we began receiving parcels of men's clothing from the United States. Every parcel that came puzzled me more than the previous one because every item appeared to be the clothing of one small man less than five feet, six inches tall. Gifford was six feet tall. Our fellow missionaries were larger men, too, so the clothing was useless for our needs. Each package contained one type of clothing such as hats, jackets, pants, shirts, and the like. The one-size-fits-all handkerchiefs were about the only items any of us could use. I could have worn the shoes; they fit me, but they were hardly appropriate.

These parcels arrived over a period of ten days. Not only were the items of no use to us, but we had to pay a handling charge on each one! It was a small fee, but to me it seemed like the last straw to have to pay for something we neither asked for, nor wanted. I remember standing in the doorway as I tossed the last parcel onto the bed and actually asking God if He was playing a joke on us. I'm thankful that God understands and forgives such rudeness. But worse than that was the unbelief regarding God's goodness that began to encrust my heart.

A day or two after the last box arrived, Gifford and I were on our knees for our daily time of prayer together. I could pray no words. Gifford simply asked the Lord to send our daily bread for that day. I tried not to think about the parcels, but as we stood up, Gifford broke into a grin. "I'll bet I can take some of those things to that used clothing store I saw on Main Street!" he exclaimed. He ran up the stairs, grabbed the box of men's shoes and started off down the street. In no time he was back without the box. Waving Japanese money in my face, he took me by the arm and said, "Let's go shopping!"

This took place in 1950, when Japan was still recuperating from the ravages of the war, and the people were glad for clothing of any kind. Gifford found a great market for all the second-hand clothing that had been sent, especially the beautiful woolen sweaters and suits. The Japanese don't bargain as a rule, but Gifford's childhood in China, where bargaining was a way of life, inspired him to get the very best price he could for each item, because everything was of high quality. Without a doubt, the Lord had allowed this clothing to be sent with the small Japanese stature in mind. Definite prayers, definite answers? Too small men's clothing hardly seemed God's definite answer to our prayer. But of course it was.

Standing atop that unusual and unexpected memorial, I have surveyed the past and given thanks many times. The highlight of this story came years later while we were on furlough. When I told that story to a ladies' missionary class in Cleveland, Ohio, an excited lady came rushing up afterward and said that those were her Uncle Tom's things. When he died, they packed up all his clothing and sent them to us. She was as thrilled in hearing the story as I had been in telling it. No wonder God tells us to "remember." Remembrance gives us confidence to look to the future as we recall the faithfulness of God in the past.

11
DOES HE HATE ME?

"He, being full of compassion, forgave their iniquity, and destroyed them not: yea, many a time turned He His anger away, and did not stir up all His wrath. For He remembered that they were but flesh."
PSALM 78:38-39

I've always loved the story of Joseph; Genesis 50:15-21 has gripped my heart many times. But when I read it recently, the Lord brought a mistaken judgment that his brothers held to my attention. I can't say that I ever saw myself quite so plainly in this little episode before:

And when Joseph's brethren saw that their father was dead, they said, Joseph will perhaps hate us, and will certainly requite us all the evil which we did unto him…and Joseph wept…And Joseph said unto them…fear ye not; I will nourish you, and your little ones. And he comforted them.

How could they possibly think that Joseph would hate them and take vengeance on them now, after having seen the wagon loads of supplies he had sent for their trip to Egypt? How could they possibly doubt him, after enjoying his provision of the best of the land for their families? How could they think he would take revenge after he had told them he forgave them, and had embraced them with tears and kisses? How could they? His brothers didn't know Joseph very well, or they would never have entertained such thoughts toward him. I can image Joseph wincing as they made their accusations,

59

pleading for mercy so unnecessarily. Their fears were a reflection on his character; they had attacked his integrity.

With some brothers such fears may have been justified, but certainly not with Joseph. He had proven otherwise in so many ways. He had given and given again. Once they had acknowledged their sin, he had forgiven them entirely.

I struggled against similar thoughts toward the Lord. I was confusing the principle of sowing and reaping with God's vindictiveness, assuming that what I was experiencing was God's judgment. I was judging God by my circumstances, not by what He reveals to me in His Word about His integrity and forgiving spirit. I had even reached the place where I wondered if God hated me.

When I read this portion in Genesis, the Lord gave me a glimpse of His grief caused by my unworthy thoughts of Him. He seemed to be saying to me that I was to stop my analysis of things as failing, sinful creatures might see things. I needed to dwell on His character, not judging Him by circumstances. The more I thought about His greatness, the more I could see that I had indeed sinned against Him by thinking He would take revenge. I could only bow my head in thanks and praise to Him. Dwelling on the wagon loads and the best of the land was much more profitable than cringing in my fear and bemoaning my unworthiness. I knew afresh that I had sinned against Him, and that I did not deserve any of His goodness, but I also saw His marvelous grace and mercy in cleansing me through Christ's blood. Of course I didn't deserve such treatment. but mercy and grace, by their very definition, are undeserved.

This encounter with God has given me a new desire to evaluate His character in the light of His Word and not in terms of what I or anyone else might do. I do Him a great injustice otherwise. How can I ever forget His words: *"Fear not, thou worm Jacob, and ye men of Israel; I will help thee, saith the Lord, and thy redeemer, the Holy One of Israel"* (Isa. 41:14).

12
FAITHFUL WITNESSES

*"All the ends of the world shall remember and turn unto the Lord:
and all the kindreds of the nations shall worship before Thee. For
the kingdom is the Lord's: and He is the governor among the
nations."*
PSALM 22:27-28

Back in the early '60s, Gifford met three unusual high
school students. He met each one individually, but soon discovered that they were brothers. He met one on a train to
Tokyo and struck up a conversation with him. Judging by the
young man's questions, it was evident that he was a deep
thinker. Gifford was so impressed that he came home and told
me about this earnest young man who seemed to be thinking
about, and searching for, God. The second brother stopped to
read the bulletin board in front of the chapel in Takasaki one
Sunday afternoon. Gifford walked up to him and asked if he
had any questions about the schedule of meetings. He had
plenty of questions, not about the schedule, but about God. I
don't remember the circumstances of our meeting the third
brother, but all of this happened within a two-week period, so
we assumed that God had something special in mind for us
and for them.

The brothers were all surprised to encounter each other in
the room of a fire station that had been rented for a weekly
Bible class. Evidently, there had been many long discussions
about spiritual things at home, and each had inspired the oth-

ers to search for answers. From the beginning it was apparent that they were from an intellectual home, a home that emphasized education to the point of creating stress. These fine young men were a real credit to their family. How they found time in their busy schedules to attend Bible classes is still surprising to me. But none of them missed the class very often, and they would stay for hours afterwards. They couldn't get enough. When the announcements for camp were distributed, their response to attend was unanimous. How they got their parents' permission was even more surprising. They attended the spring camp session; and two of them, if I remember correctly, were saved that week. The Lord had prepared their hearts before they came to the Bible class, and their faithful attendance paved the way for a wholehearted response to the gospel.

One Sunday night, within the first year of acquaintance with these brothers, the door to the chapel squeaked open. I glanced back to see who was coming in late and noticed that there was something unusual about the dignified, middle-aged gentleman who had walked in. Most of the audience in that stage of our work was comprised of students, but this man walked in like he had always attended. He took a seat and listened to the message with earnestness, just as comfortable as if he were one of the students. After the service, while everyone was having tea together, the three brothers introduced the newcomer as their father. He certainly looked worthy of that position.

Needless to say, the boys were surprised to see him there, and so were we. We expected to hear the usual complaint that his sons were spending too much time at the classes and the meetings on Sunday, but to our surprise, that was not his purpose for attending that evening. When Gifford asked him what brought him to the service, he gave the following story as an explanation.

He said that he had seen a change in his sons and wanted

to know how it came about. He explained that his boys were all born within thirteen months. The oldest son was only thirteen months old when the twins were born, and ever since birth they had seemed to be rivals. Although we had never seen this side of them, they were always in competition with each other at home, often arguing with each other. The father said that this attitude had stopped since they had spent a week at camp, and that he had come to find out what had made this great difference. He wanted to know what had changed them to live peacefully together.

When he stopped speaking, you could have heard the proverbial pin drop. It was hard to tell who was the most pleased with his observation—the sons or we. Gifford lost no time in giving the Lord His rightful credit in having power to change people's lives. The father ended his visit with an invitation for us to visit him in his home.

The father later told us that while he was a medical student, he had rented a room in a home where the host father talked about Jesus dying on the cross to take away our sins. At the time he was too occupied to give it much thought, but that as he listened to us, he had been remembering some of the things his host had told him about the power of God. He also recalled that his host had told him that if he ever felt he was lacking something in his life, to seek out someone who could help him understand more about the Bible and the reason for the cross of Christ.

As a result of the combination of the faithful witness of this dear saint of God and the visit to the home, a cottage meeting was started in his home, which was about an hour's drive from the chapel. He was an extremely popular doctor, and couldn't attend services on most Sundays because he was on call. He could arrange to be free on Tuesday nights except for emergencies. I don't remember many of the details of the cottage meetings in their home those first few years, but I do remember signing the mother up to attend the Billy Graham

Crusade four years later.

One hundred eighteen people had registered to go into Tokyo to attend the crusade, five people over the capacity of the buses. I decided to drive in separately. I followed the buses, praying the whole way for the doctor's wife. She went forward that night. It is vivid in my memory because the whole hundred and eighteen people had to wait afterwards. The bus drivers were not particularly happy, but we certainly were. Her salvation was as clear a case as her sons' had been.

Following the crusade, the four saved family members pled to God for the father who was having a real struggle. He had no doubt about the truth of what he was hearing, but he was not quite ready to pay the price for being a Christian in his community. He was counting the cost and he knew it would be high.

A few nights after the wife received Christ, I went to Tokyo for a crusade meeting alone. When I was riding the train back to Takasaki, I met the doctor himself, also alone. The fact that we were riding in the same car of a train carrying over a thousand people was no coincidence. We had no idea until much later what had been holding the doctor back from making an open confession of faith in Jesus Christ as his Saviour.

His struggle centered on a problem familiar to the Japanese: what to do with the family shrines. Not only did they have the family shrine in their home, but they had a small shrine in their garden, and a large community shrine in the corner of their property. As the oldest son in the family, he was responsible for maintaining the worship of the ancestral line. He had inherited not only his father's clinic and home, but the ancestral rituals as well. His responsibility included overseeing all the daily offerings, and rites on special occasions—especially at festival times. He would be destroying family property if he did away with them.

When his older sister learned that he was interested in becoming a Christian, she gave him no peace. She reminded him of his obligations, arguing that this was not a personal matter because it concerned the whole family, past and future generations. There was so much at stake that it is impossible to explain all the complications. Although there were many possible solutions to his problem, he did not want to compromise. At the same time he was not ready to destroy the shrines, either.

Others in a similar situation may have simply turned these objects over to another family member, but he believed that, according to Deuteronomy 7:25-26, they were cursed by God. Why turn a cursed object over to another? He was convicted that he was responsible to completely destroy these shrines himself. But could he?

The graven images of their gods shall ye burn with fire; thou shalt not desire the silver or gold that is on them, nor take it unto thee, lest thou be snared therein; for it is an abomination to the Lord thy God. Neither shalt thou bring an abomination into thine house lest thou be a cursed thing like it, but thou shalt utterly detest it, thou shalt abhor it, for it is a cursed thing.

He struggled with this issue for another three years! Believe me, Gifford and I struggled along with him. We easily could have said what we believed he should do. However, since practically all Japanese Christians face this same issue, we knew that the final decision must be his. His sons knew it, too. Only the power of God enables Christians to deal with such opposition. The incentive and ability to please the Lord must come from the heart, as inspired by the Holy Spirit.

It is impossible for me to pinpoint the time of his salvation, but we soon noticed there was a difference in his life. He was able to make arrangements so he could attend the meetings almost every Sunday. Then we noticed that the doors of the family shrine were closed and there was no incense burning before the gold-plated tablet with the names of the ancestors engraved on it. But to actually burn it! A drastic step!

We had scheduled a baptism on a particular Sunday morning, and none of the boys were at the service when we started. This was unusual, so we were concerned. After we sang a few opening songs, the doctor walked in, leading his family. One glance at his beaming face told us that something wonderful had happened. He couldn't hold the news in. He shared with us all that he and his sons had held a service in their garden and had burned the shrines. What victory! What joy we all shared together. It is impossible to describe the spirit of celebration that morning as we remembered the Lord together. Later, he announced that he was now ready to be baptized as his wife and sons had been. The elders all knew how long he had battled with this step of following the Lord, and were happy to baptize him on the confession of his faith.

This family's history stands as a faithful witness to Romans 11:22—"*Behold, therefore the goodness and severity of God...*"

As to God's severity, many times during the doctor's years of struggle, we were tempted to think that God was perhaps a bit too severe in demanding allegiance to Himself alone, severe in making His people choose to believe that He is who He says He is. At times it appeared that God was testing this dear man and his wife more than they could bear, but God knew that he could take the testing and that he would grow quickly through it. Although he was in his mid-fifties, he learned as quickly as his student sons had learned the basics of the spiritual life.

As for God's goodness, it was very apparent to me when I visited their home two years ago that God had indeed blessed them. At this special gathering, their children and grandchildren were all present; every one of the adults professes to know Christ as Saviour. This man did not lose respect in the community. He became busier than ever. His older sister had been angry for a time, but in her later years, she will allow no other physician to attend her, although she herself is not saved. She trusts her brother implicitly because she respects his judgment.

The Lord's goodness has extended to the next generation. Each of the doctor's sons married a Christian woman. The oldest son, also an M.D., owns and operates a home for the aged. The second son has taken over his father's practice, and has built a home adjacent to his parents' home. Although the father is well into his eighties, he still acts as an advisor to both of these sons. The third son is a school teacher who uses his position to serve the Lord in an unusual way. I can only bow my head in adoration to the great God who stands behind all that He promises in His Word.

13
FOUR GENERATIONS

"Therefore it shall be, when the Lord thy God hath given thee rest from all thine enemies round about...that thou shalt blot out the remembrance of Amalek from under heaven; thou shalt not forget it."
DEUTERONOMY 25:19

I derive great pleasure from remembering chains of events, trying to recall which event followed which, and finding joy in rediscovering how the preaching of the cross has been used as the power of God unto salvation. This morning, as I traced one series of events that led to salvation of four generations, I longed for the old days of tent meetings.

There was much involved in conducting a tent meeting. The setting up of the tent was an event in itself. Then someone would need to sleep there each night to guard the place and equipment. Meals had to be prepared to feed the people who helped. The speaker and all his guests had to be entertained. Plus we had to be ready to provide hours of personal counseling, for those tent meetings were always well attended. Memories of these events brought joy to my heart. I remembered watching God work in the lives of people, seeing how the conviction of sin brought repentance, which in turn brought the joy of being born again. This world offers nothing that causes such great rejoicing.

The memory of one woman who was touched by the message of salvation put my mind into high gear. Why this dear woman had even attended the tent meeting puzzles me, because we later learned that she lived a good hour away from the area. We do know why she made the same trip the following morning to visit us, however. She had a heavy burden for her aged mother, who was desperately sick at the time. Why she was not concerned for her own soul but only for that of her mother was an even greater puzzle. Gifford had spoken the night before from John 3:3,

> *Verily, verily I say unto thee, Except a man be born again, he cannot see the kingdom of God.*

I can still see the urgency in her face as she pled with Gifford to make the return trip home with her. She wanted her mother to hear how to be born again before she died. Her mother wanted to go to heaven. Her loving concern for her mother was very touching. Gifford sensed an opportunity to meet the family as well as to talk to her mother, so made arrangements to clear the schedule, and promised to visit the elderly lady.

If my memory serves me right, the mother was eighty-six years old. She was bedridden and very sick. The family gave Gifford a warm welcome, and he found the aged woman herself very receptive to the gospel. She was alert and well prepared by the Holy Spirit; she literally soaked up the message of the cross of Christ. She admitted she was a sinner—the concept of sin is usually very difficult for the Japanese to grasp, and especially for elderly people, but she had no problem with it. She knew she was not righteous enough to enter heaven. If she needed to be born again, she wanted to know how that took place.

Gifford's visit was the beginning of a monthly cottage meeting. Out of respect to the grandmother, the grandchildren would join them. The grandmother was the first to be saved; two of her daughters, including the one who had invited him, soon followed, and Gifford had high hopes for the grandchildren. At first there was great attendance, but it settled down to two grandsons who showed the most interest. They came regularly. The grandmother began to improve in health and lived six years afterwards. She was not just a spiritual spectator, she was very involved. One of her grandsons later revealed that they feared her prayers. They would lie in the next room at night and hear her praying for them, name by name (the rice paper sliding doors between rooms made this possible).

After graduating from high school, one of the grandsons got a position in a factory located about halfway between our home and his. Gifford would pick him up after work, take him to his grandmother's for the meeting, and drop him off on the way back. He lived in the men's dorm of the factory at the time, and on many nights he really didn't want to go. He would make himself scarce, but Gifford was not easily discouraged; he would find him and encourage him to go with him. Eventually, he too, was saved. The camp played a large place in the spiritual growth of these two grandsons. They began going with Gifford, and helping in other meetings here and there as well.

I don't remember that the family shrine was a difficult problem in that home because the grandmother was very clear in her decisions. Neither did she fear the retaliation of the spirits of her ancestors. Since there were no adult men in the house, her word was law. She reasoned that if God hated these representations of heathen gods, she should too. Over time, the offerings became conspicuous by their absence. Then we noticed that the doors of the shrine were shut as it sat on the shelf. The climax came when the two boys hauled it up to camp and it became fuel for one of the warmest and happiest campfire we ever had.

That campfire stands out as a memorial to the power of God. As the match was lit and the shrine started to burn, a hush fell over the assembled young people. The campers were appalled that such a thing could be happening in Buddhist

Japan. There was a feeling of fear that some great catastrophe would surely strike. Then the victory of the moment was realized and we all burst out into song. Testimonies followed well into the night, as the ashes gave visible evidence of the total victory that comes with obedience to God's Word. Another representation of false gods had gone down in defeat, a foretaste of that day when every enemy of God will be put down, and His King shall rule supreme.

Eventually we got news that the grandmother was failing fast, I went one evening to see her. While I was there, the doctor came and wanted to give her an injection. She asked him not to, saying that she really would rather go to be with Jesus. He mumbled something about the fact that he was duty-bound to give it to her, so he gave the injection and left. That evening, even before I reached home, she slipped into the presence of the Lord whom she had learned to love so dearly.

However, her death did not end her verbal testimony to her extended family. Before she died, she made a tape that she requested be played at her funeral. When the tape was played, there wasn't a dry eye in the audience. She presented the message of the cross. To many, it was foolishness, but to one grandson, it was the power of God. One of the two who were saved, he had wandered away from God and His people. The urgency of her talk, and the earnestness of her plea—that we all face the truth that one day we will stand before the Lord and give account—brought him to his knees in conviction of sin and back to the fellowship of the saints where he has consistently been for more than twenty years.

As I put all these thoughts together, I can tell you that her testimony has now reached down to the fourth generation. The seed has multiplied many-fold as a number of her great-grandchildren are now born again and in fellowship with believers. All this is the result of one series of tent meetings—and God, the God who uses weak things to confound the mighty and next-to-nothing things to accomplish His will.

14
FATHER'S DAY GIFT

"One generation shall praise Thy works to another, and shall declare Thy mighty acts...They shall abundantly utter the memory of Thy great goodness, and shall sing of Thy righteousness."
PSALM 145:4, 7

My heavenly Father woke me this morning at 4 A.M. with the most wonderful thought I've had all year. I fell asleep again with this precious truth filling my mind. Two hours later, He nudged me with a more urgent message: "Get up and write," He seemed to say. "Put this down on paper before the thrill of it fades."

What was the thought? It was that my Father gave *me* a Father's Day gift instead of vice versa, and with this thought He impressed two verses indelibly on my heart:

...I will receive you, and will be a Father unto you, and ye shall be My sons and daughters, saith the Lord Almighty (2 Cor. 6:17-18).

I've known for years that God was my Father, but the thought came in a very special way this morning as I suddenly realized that my special gift came on Father's Day. What was the gift I received from my heavenly Father? It was a brand new 1996 Caravan! I, who could never tell one car from another, except by color—(Gifford used to test me as we drove along by asking me the different makes of car. I could only say, "You'll have to get closer; I can't read it.")—I now own a vehi-

73

cle that is the idol of many a man. It is worth noting that this wonderful gift from the Lord was made possible by three fathers, all of whom played a vital part in its purchase.

The first father was my earthly father. I can't explain why the Lord gave me the earthly father He did, but as I thought of him this morning, I was overcome with gratefulness. When my life began seventy-four years ago, my father was not saved. However, he was a good man who married a great woman. I look back with deep thanksgiving to the day my father was born again. The whole family knew something had happened, although at the time my mother didn't appreciate the abrupt halt to their parties! It took her a whole year to see what Dad had seen, and to receive the same salvation in which he found such joy.

The second father the Lord used was my father-in-law. As I thought about him, I had the same reaction—a deep feeling of debt to the Lord for bringing me into a devoted, stable, missionary family. The life example of my in-laws, especially Dad, was a constant positive challenge to me.

The third father was the father of my own three daughters. Nothing I could write would adequately express how I feel about him and our life together, nor would it properly convey my thanks to God for giving him to me. The memory of seeing his wedding ring reflect in the light during the first sermon I heard him preach after we were married tells it all, "He's mine!" A loving, godly husband is a rich treasure indeed.

The capstone to this memorial that prompted me to put this down on paper was the reassuring passage above, given in a special way to me this morning. It was given to me by God, the God who created fathers in His image, who is my Everlasting Father. During the past twenty years, I have often found encouragement in the way the Lord literally fulfilled His promise to care for all three of the above-mentioned fathers and their spouses until He took them to Himself. All three of these men sought the kingdom of God and His righteousness first. Each had as his mission in life to be a holy man of God, often making huge sacrifices for the sake of the Lord. I bear witness to the truth that the Lord added to them, to their mates, and to their children all the necessities of life.

The story of my new van is a continuation of that promise, and it actually started way back—more than thirty years ago—when my mother and dad bought a house in Florida. He knew that he was sick and that he might not have many more years left to care for my mother. So he took out the longest loan with the smallest payment possible so that it would not put too great a strain on their finances. This detail was important when I took over the responsibility of making Mom's house payments years ago.

After Dad died, mother managed very well. But the day came when some provision for her care financially was necessary. I was talking over the situation with my father-in-law, and he suggested that I buy Mom's house, a very modest one, and put a Quit Claim on it. This would assure her of a roof over her head for as long as she lived, and because I was making the monthly payment, I would be preparing a place for myself when I would retire. The plan sounded reasonable to me, but there was the bothersome matter of the missing down payment. I never mentioned this to Gifford's dad, but he took me into the study one afternoon and handed me a check. He told me that he had been praying for my mother and for me, and believed that the Lord wanted him to take action by providing the down payment and lawyer's fees.

When the time came for me to return to the United States, my mother was still well and living in her little home, so I settled in the Denver area where I had two daughters. To make a long story short, my mother passed away, her home was sold—and my old van was giving me trouble. I began shopping around for a newer vehicle. I almost put a deposit on a good, used van, but for some reason I couldn't give the final word. The dealer had shown me a new one, but there was a substantial difference between the money in hand and the price of the new van.

A few days later, an unexpected gift arrived from several of Gifford's spiritual sons in Japan. Everything came together perfectly. A friend who had been advising me in this shopping for a car took me by to see a new van on a car lot one Sunday afternoon. He had been talking to a dealer. We decided, "This is it!" I committed myself verbally to return the following morning to finish the deal. This morning I realized that the day the decision was made was Father's Day.

So the thoughtfulness of my own father in helping to provide that house in Florida, the generosity of my father-in-law in giving the down payment for its purchase some years later, and a return on the spiritual investment Gifford made in the lives of some Japanese believers, all came together in a visible expression of the faithful provision of our heavenly Father. A van on Father's Day!

15
GOD GIVES FUZZIES

"He hath made His wonderful works to be remembered: the Lord is gracious and full of compassion."
PSALM 111:4

When I think of "fuzzies," I think of those pleasant surprises the Lord loves to give us that create a warm feeling, a contented sense of well-being, like curling up with a warm, fuzzy blanket on a cold winter's night. "Fuzzies" are different with each individual. They wouldn't be classified as necessities. These are things we can easily do without, but they add that special touch to life. The thought of the extras that God has so often sent my way really keeps my heart warm. Yes, God gives "fuzzies." Lots of them! As the Psalmist wrote:

How precious also are Thy thoughts unto me, O God! How great is the sum of them. If I should count them, they are more in number than the sand (Ps. 139:17-18).

One such thoughtful detail was the color of my van. I've already told you about the van. Up to a point, the van is a necessity to me for the Bible classes, but the color was a bonus. When I saw it in the parking lot, the price was a thrill, but the color really appealed to me. It seemed to say, "This is it."

Another special touch came soon after Gifford went to be with the Lord. I was still in a state of shock, when a dear friend arranged for me to return to the United States to spend some time with my daughters who were also adjusting to their father's death. Plans were made for me which included a three-day stop in Hawaii. It should have been one of those special extras which our heavenly Father loves to give, but I was not really looking forward to it. I was more or less in a stupor, being moved along by a force outside myself. I had no idea what I would do in Hawaii, for I knew no one there.

But the Lord had a family meet me that was definitely suited to my needs at that time. The things they said reached my aching heart, and they took me into their family as one of them. They far exceeded any expectations I had. Within hours, we were one in spirit and I felt loved in a very special sense. Their spiritual outlook warmed my heart and gave me new hope for my future as a widow. Only God knows the difference those few days made in preparation for meeting my girls in their sorrow.

Another loving detail comes to mind as one of the ways God decorates our lives. About two years later, I had returned to Japan and had settled into my new routine. I sorted out things and started using Gifford's large desk as my own—all but his top drawer where he kept his most personal things. I just couldn't make myself go through it because I was sure there were just too many items of sentimental value in there.

However, at the advice of a friend, I decided one day to plunge in, sort through and throw away things I didn't have use for myself. I was making good progress when I noticed an eyeglasses case shoved up against the back. I didn't recognize it, but when I opened the case and pulled out the object wrapped in tissue, I held in my hand a pair of glasses with a simple notation: these were the eyeglasses I had been wearing when Gifford and I met each other thirty-three years before.

He had carried these glasses out of China when we were evacuated, into Taiwan, and later carried them into Japan—purely for sentimental reasons. Seeing this unexpected reminder of Gifford's love released a flood of tears that I had been fighting so hard to keep under control. It brought an unbelievable sense of relief sorely needed at that time.

It was some time after moving into our home in the Denver area that I remembered a passage of Scripture that the Lord had given to me while still in Japan. It mentioned that when Abraham bought the cave of Mach-pelah (Gen. 23), it included the field of Ephron. The purchase of the field is stated to include "all the trees that were in the field." Abraham was just looking for a place to bury the dead; God gave him a symbol of life and growth and future potential.

The day this "fuzzy" came to mind I was sitting out on the patio drinking a cup of tea. The birds were singing so heartily in the trees, and as I enjoyed them, I thought of this passage again. It was as if the Lord said, "When you bought this place, did you notice the trees?" The trees and birds have often been a delight to me since that day. I could live happily without being surrounded by these lovely, big trees, but God, in His goodness, had them planted years before. They are now a special gift to remind me that He is aware of what I have to enjoy. Our God gives us *richly* all things to enjoy (1 Tim. 6:17).

Take time out to bask in the warmth of your "fuzzies." Delight in knowing that the Lord cares about *you* in a special way today.

16
THE GOD OF PATIENCE

"Remembering without ceasing your work of faith, and labor of love, and patience of hope in our Lord Jesus Christ, in the sight of God and our Father."
1 THESSALONIANS 1:3

One afternoon, a very anxious and troubled wife and mother visited us. Her request was a good one, one that we quickly granted. Her husband had just been admitted to a tuberculosis sanitarium and was threatening suicide. She wanted us to visit him. The sanitarium was a couple of hours from us in the mountains, but with an urgent request like this, we soon arranged to go.

The visit became a monthly one, and later turned into a Bible study. The young man was initially very receptive to the gospel, and we had high hopes for his salvation. His interest was certainly the tool God used to get us into the hospital. However, the Lord, who knows the end from the beginning, had a different but wonderful plan in mind for our visits. Soon after the Bible class started, a young lady began to attend. It clearly was for her benefit that the class continued after the man we first visited was released and returned home to Takasaki. We helped him move back home, but his interest in the matters concerning eternal life vanished when he got back on his feet and returned to work. Needless to say, this was a great disappointment to us.

Our friendship with the young woman, however, blossomed. A few years later, she accepted Christ through the Bible studies. Her faith grew by leaps and bounds while she was hospitalized, and became even stronger when she was released about five years later.

This young woman was the only child of a widow who worked hard to keep body and soul together. Even so, they lived in very poor quarters. I visited the mother one Sunday afternoon and was most surprised at the open opposition I felt from her. She told me in no uncertain terms that we were to leave her daughter alone. She informed me that they had their own religion and didn't need our "foreign" one. I was surprised for two reasons: first, the young lady had not told me how her mother opposed her faith; second, the mother's outburst was contrary to typical Japanese culture. It was the first time during our years in Japan that I was spoken to as frankly as she talked to me that afternoon. I was nonplussed and didn't stay very long. From that visit, we realized that our dear friend needed the support of her fellow believers more than ever, so we increased our prayers for her.

We were amazed when our friend arrived at the meeting the following Sunday all smiling, her face aglow. I expected to hear that her mother had given in, but instead her mother had complained the whole week about her leaving her with all the housework. She was extremely angry that her daughter would oppose her wishes and come to the chapel, yet, even with all this, the daughter had peace and joy. It was rare for a Japanese girl to go against her mother like this.

The daughter had arisen early enough to get the wash done and on the clothes line before she went to the meeting, and she returned home immediately after the service. She continued to come every Sunday for years, without fail. Seldom have I ever seen such Christian character and determination in action. I was afraid for her health because this put pressure on her weakened body.

Her mother gradually settled down and accepted this

arrangement, although she continued her complaining that her daughter would leave her alone for half a day on Sundays. She never softened in her opposition to the change in "religion," and took it as a personal affront from her daughter to have left the family religion.

Although her health was a concern, the daughter did not fail under the extra load of work. In fact, her health steadily improved to the place that she was able to take a part-time job, helping her mother with the finances as well. For years I drove this young sister back home to save her strength.

After some years, the mother softened a little. One day she ventured out to the car to thank me for my kindness to her daughter, and later even came with her daughter to visit us.

After the girl's health improved, the mother began speaking of marriage. She was worried about her own future and the girl's as well. She arranged for a middle-man to search for a husband for her daughter. However, the girl refused to even speak of marriage plans to the men who were suggested; she was adamant that she would not marry an unbeliever. The single status of the girl remained a bone of contention for years and unfortunately, no available Christian bachelors were to be found.

It was only the grace of God that kept the dear soul from capitulating under the combination of the pressure of the world around her, her desire from within, and the manipulation of Satan to bring it all about. The mother persuaded their family members and circle of friends to talk "some sense" into her. She was middle-aged by this time. Yet God by His Spirit developed in her that strength of character needed to endure in the Lord—not a matter of months, but years.

Eventually the daughter retired from her job. At about the same time, the manager of our Christian bookstore had to move from the apartment over the shop and the salesperson had to quit as well. At the prayer-meeting one week, there were two prayer requests: one that our sister would have guidance as to their future because she and her mother had to vacate their apartment: second, for a salesperson to take over the store. We had been so terribly disappointed and puzzled over the turn of events, but on hearing these requests together, there were five people present who had the same idea. Was this the plan of God developing before our eyes?

The bookstore manager and his wife, Gifford and I, and the sister in question all saw it coming. Each, however, was afraid to mention it to the other parties. Each went home to pray about our thoughts and to ask God to lead in His way. We all knew how complicated it could be to expect the mother to move over a "Christian" bookstore. We had limited God, because as soon as the idea was brought out into the open, we all had the assurance that this was very much of the Lord. Even the mother agreed—though not too happily—to the plan that her daughter work in the store and they move into the apartment over the shop. By supplementing the low bookstore salary with her retirement money, and living in the apartment free of charge, they would have a good living arrangement. Many were the prayers of thanksgiving in seeing God's perfect plan for all concerned.

At first, the mother stayed upstairs all day long, but she soon grew tired of that, and began to visit the shop for short intervals. She found the customers to be pleasant and friendly. All the believers knew the situation and prayed for this dear lady. In time, being bored, she began picking up books and reading them. She was fascinated by a certain children's book with lovely pictures. She had poor eyesight, but found that she could read the large print. She would run her fingers down the page, laboriously reading the Bible stories.

One afternoon, she read the story of Christ's crucifixion. Tears began to trickle down her cheeks until she didn't even try to control them. Being the only other person in the store, her daughter went over to her, and asked what was troubling her. The mother looked up and, in all earnestness, asked, "Did the Lord die for me, too? Would He really do that for me when I have been so mean and hateful?"

Of course, the answer was, "Yes, Mother!" That day the mother prayed with her daughter and was gloriously saved. Although she was into her eighties, she asked for baptism and became a faithful and earnest sister in the Lord.

She appointed herself to keep the front of the shop swept and clean. She also found a three-foot space all along the back wall of the store where she could plant vegetables. The plot had a southern exposure and, aided by her "green thumb," everything grew beautifully. She was so happy when she could pick the first fruit and ceremoniously bring it to me, not under some religious obligation, but out of a heart of genuine love. I felt like I was eating sacred cucumbers, tomatoes, and green beans, a harvest like the old woman herself, that had required patient care and sunshine to bring it to fruition. When I think of all that transpired because of the faithful patience and love of one Japanese daughter, I am reminded of Romans 15:5-6:

> Now the God of patience and consolation grant you to be like-minded one toward another according to Christ Jesus: that ye may with one mind and one mouth glorify God, even the Father of our Lord Jesus Christ.

17
GOD'S MYSTERIOUS WAYS

"When I call to remembrance the unfeigned faith that is in thee,
which dwelt first in thy grandmother Lois, and thy mother Eunice;
and I am persuaded that in thee also."
2 TIMOTHY 1:5

I am aware of three local churches in Japan that were built largely because of the influence of sisters in the Lord. All three are flourishing assemblies of strong Christian families, and are built on a solid spiritual foundation. All show Christ as Head—not only of His invisible church, but of the local church as well. Yet none of these women stepped out of the pattern of male leadership in the church. I greatly admire these sisters because I can imagine a few of the frustrations and doubts that they must have had to deal with at times.

In two cases, the foundation for these assemblies was laid through children's work, and later as a result of discussions around a dining room table. The third church was started because a medical student wanted English instruction; he later was saved. He in turn reached out to a classmate with the gospel, and through that contact cottage meetings began.

I watched two of these gatherings develop from a distance, but I saw the third one firsthand through a bit of personal involvement. The history of all three started more than thirty years ago. I have great joy in sitting back and thinking about what the Lord has done. God's patience, and the patience of the people He used in the establishment of these churches, is worthy of our consideration. Allow me to focus on the seemingly insignificant beginnings of the third assembly.

During those cottage meetings where the medical student was saved, a second student confessed Christ. Both students were baptized in our backyard pool nearly forty years ago. About the time these young people came to the Lord, Gifford started helping in a new work that was about a four-hour drive from Takasaki. He traveled there once a month, and since the home of the second student was on the way, he stopped there for a visit. He received a warm welcome and an invitation to visit again. These visits continued for several months, and through that contact the student's younger sister became a Christian.

In time, friends and family were invited to these Bible studies. Rich fellowship grew into precious friendships as the sisters showed genuine Christian hospitality to all who came. But best of all, God was obviously working in their hearts, for interest grew as other members of the family confessed Christ as Saviour and Lord. With their response, it soon became apparent that getting together once a month was not enough.

They began inviting other missionaries and evangelists to stop and teach whenever they were in the vicinity. Tapes were made of these messages and played repeatedly between visits. In the meantime, the sisters began driving a good distance every week to attend an assembly where upbuilding ministry helped them to develop. Their spiritual growth was amazing as the seedlings continually sent their roots deeper.

As more people attended the group, it became plain that the Lord had His hand of blessing on these believers. Everyone involved felt that the time had come to begin planting another local church for His glory. Many had a hand in this: a college student who returned home for employment after graduation; a man who chose to accept a job in the area and move his family there for the express purpose of helping; a Japanese evangelist who regularly drove there. By the Spirit's work through these faithful servants, many people were added to the fellowship. The student, who is now a doctor with her own clinic, had a good testimony in the community and among her nursing staff, so she attracted others to examine the claims of Christ and His pattern for the church.

When I accepted an invitation to speak at a special ladies' meeting at this assembly during my recent visit to Japan, I realized that I had not kept up with the growth there. I took for granted that the meeting would be held at the original cottage meeting site with which I was familiar. I was not prepared to be driven up to a lovely, new-looking building. Nor did I envision speaking to so many more new sisters than had attended during my last visit many years before. The small group I had known had grown and matured. They had renovated an old warehouse, put a new face on it, and turned it into a functional chapel.

I always have been weak when it comes to keeping my composure in the face of happy surprises, so, as usual, I had a difficult time holding back the tears of joy. I had a feeling of great awe as I tried to take it all in. All I could do was say a quick, "Thank You, Lord!" and gratefully accept the warm welcome I received. This was one more confirmation that we serve a great God! That assembly stands as a monument to God's power in working—contrary to the normal pattern.

At the risk of letting my imagination run away with me, I picture the faces of these dear sisters and see their joy as they receive a crown from the hand of the Chief Shepherd. Will He not say to them, "Well done, good and faithful servants; enter thou into the joy of thy Lord." What a thrill they will have to be rewarded in everlasting joy! Their faith has not only pleased Him, their joy already has been great, but they have yet to be abundantly rewarded for their faithful service to Him (Heb. 11:6). Of each of them it can be said, "She hath done what she could"(Mk. 14:8). Can it also be said of me and of you?

18
HOW TO PICK A FIANCÉ

*"Wherefore I will not be negligent to put you always in
remembrance of these things, though ye know them, and be
established in the present truth."*
2 PETER 1:12

Through the years, I have seen many Christian women
marry—some for better, and some for worse. So I have a few
suggestions for any bride-to-be. Before the wedding bells ring,
make sure your choice of a husband is the right one.

Paul approaches the subject of married life with the words,
"Submitting yourselves one to another in the fear of God"
(Eph. 5:21). As far as I'm concerned, there are two very impor-
tant thoughts to note in this verse.

First, the hands you will be placing your life into should be
the hands of a man who truly fears God. That is where the
whole issue lies. You want a man of integrity. You want a man
who walks righteously before God at all times. You want to
live your life with a man who is conscious that "the eyes of the
Lord move to and fro throughout the whole earth to show
Himself strong on behalf of those whose heart is perfect
toward Him." If a man fears God and wants to please Him,
that is a big step in his favor. There should be many opportunities to see evidence of this before marriage, but the trouble is
we are often blinded by infatuation, and don't catch the warn-
ing signals. A person who tries to get by with things, things
that are not quite right, is not a good candidate. Neither is a

man who brags about cheating on taxes, business deals, speeding, or the like. How could you trust a man like that?

Second, you want a man who is humble enough to submit himself to you, too. Marriage is based on give and take. The Lord, through Paul, speaks of "submitting yourselves one to another." This is important because at times you will be able to help him avoid a pitfall by making a suggestion that he may have overlooked. If he is not willing to accept this, or not able to apologize when he knows he has been wrong, you will be joining this man on a dangerous journey through life. So, think carefully before you say, "I do."

I remember two definite occasions when my husband and I disagreed on an issue and I politely (at least I think I was), told him that I believed he was wrong in his judgment, but that in obedience to the Lord's wishes I would submit to him. Later, when my husband came to me and admitted that he had been wrong and asked for my forgiveness, my estimation of my dear husband sky-rocketed. It strengthened my love for him in a way very few things have.

It is also important that we agree with Paul's admonition, "Wives, submit yourselves unto your own husbands, as unto the Lord." If we do not believe that the final decisions and responsibility for the family are to be made by the husband, we are sure to face rough times ahead. If a woman understands that God had a definite purpose in mind when He commanded this, and if she submits herself because the Lord has told her to do so, she will find joy and peace in submission. Of course, we are not advocating that wives sin in order to please their husbands. These situations are rare, but in those cases, "We ought to obey God rather than men" (Acts 5:29).

We are wise to remember that submission and trust go hand in hand. How can you fully yield yourself and your will to a person whom you cannot trust implicitly? Thus you had better think and pray long and hard before you agree to marry a man whom you cannot trust perfectly with your, and your children's, welfare. You must be confident that he is trustworthy, open and truthful, thoughtful, and that he is looking out for your good at all times, rather than putting his wishes first. Many a wife has found to her great disappointment that it is very difficult to live with a husband who puts himself first, who does only what is profitable or comfortable to him, and who operates in accordance with his whims. I pray that you never know the extreme frustration of having your life governed by the frequently changing moods of a self-centered spouse.

Another pitfall that should be avoided and can by detected before marriage, is that your future husband labors under the delusion that God holds him responsible to make you submit. If he has this attitude, he has forgotten that this matter is between you and the Lord. At the same time, you must not demand that he love you, either, because that matter is also between his heart and the Lord. The Lord, through Paul, gave these commandments directly to the spouse in each case, not for the spouse to be responsible to see that the other party carries through. So many ill feelings could be avoided if both parties kept this truth in mind.

Many will say that finding all these qualities in one man is impossible. But it isn't, really. He doesn't have to fully measure up to all these standards the day you take your vows, but he must be aware of God's purpose for him, and must be willing to work on the qualities that are still lacking. You should be able to read together what the Bible says about your roles and admit the lack. You should also understand the nature and qualities of love found in 1 Corinthians 13. This is the secret to bearing with the other in the times when we are not all we ought to be. But love goes on believing that God's love will triumph: "Love never fails."

You will find that you are lacking in certain qualities, too. But this should not be a problem as you ask the Holy Spirit to work in your lives together and produce the fruit of the Spirit there. An excellent example of a model fiancé is Joseph, Mary's husband. He stuck by his Mary even through the attack on her character; the criticism must have been fierce. He submitted to anything the Lord required of him. I pray that you will find such a man, and that your home will be a memorial to God's wondrous love.

19
IF I AM BEREAVED, I AM BEREAVED

"Like as a father pitieth his children, so the Lord pitieth them that
fear Him. For He knoweth our frame;
He remembereth that we are dust."
PSALM 103:13-14

Can you feel the pathos in Jacob's voice as he uttered, "If I am bereaved, I am bereaved" (Gen. 43:14)? As I read these words, I want to reach out, take the dear old man in my arms, and hug him. He's already suffered so much; now he faces a new loss. He has to decide to relinquish a son in order to save the lives of his children and grandchildren. You might say that he had it coming, but that doesn't make the situation any better. The pain is no less.

The ruler of Egypt had demanded that Jacob's youngest son go down to Egypt as the prerequisite for buying food. If Jacob refused to let Benjamin go, they would all die of starvation. At the time of his decision, he had no idea that by giving up the pride and joy of his life he would gain the son he had lost so many years before. It was a long, hard battle for him to be able to say that if he lost Benjamin, too, the loss would be overwhelming. Even though he said it in dejection and pessimism, the decision spelled victory although he didn't know it then.

Had Jacob remembered his son Joseph's dreams of long ago, God would have had the opportunity to give him a ray of hope, but his mind was completely occupied by the misery at hand. Had he not lost sight of the promise to his son, Joseph, that the whole family would one day bow down before him, he'd have been able to receive encouragement that Joseph was still alive. However, the fulfillment of those dreams seemed to be an impossibility. Jacob did not see God working behind the scenes.

Even though Jacob was not cooperating with God very joyfully, at least he had come to the place of yieldedness. This was the climax of a lifetime of struggle. From this point on, God was free to work. God had been waiting for this work of submission in Jacob's heart. God was also working in Joseph's life and in the lives of the eleven brothers. God was waiting to be gracious to them all. He was preparing Joseph for the foretold position of honor, and he was bringing the brothers to conviction of sin and the willingness to confess it. When His work in each life was accomplished, He was free to reveal His great glory by bringing together all the pieces of His wonderful plan.

God has a special love for all of His children. He doesn't want any of them to be hurt or lost in the refining process. Yet the process often seems painful to us. Moses, for example, had asked to see the glory of God, but God put him in a cleft of the rock, instead (Ex. 33:18-23). I'm sure Jacob also felt like he was stuck in a dark, cold frustrating cave. But, like Moses, Jacob also could see God's glory after God removed His hand and let him see what was past.

If Jacob had treasured and unflinchingly claimed the promises of God, he would have been spared years of heartache and trouble. There is great value in believing God's promises (see Heb. 11:33). The Holy Spirit lists great triumphs such as conquering countries, fighting lions, quenching fires, and escaping battles, but right in the middle of the verse, the Holy Spirit holds up the virtue of obtaining promises and hanging onto them tenaciously. If Jacob had faithfully treasured Joseph's dream in his heart (as I believe his son did), he could have had the assurance that God was in control and would bring his family together again.

Christ gave us the formula for victorious life in the midst of difficult times when He said to Martha, "Said I not unto thee that, if thou wouldest believe, thou shouldest see the glory of God?" (Jn. 11:40). With God, believing always comes before the glory. His formula is opposite that of the natural mind, which says, "If I see...I'll believe."

Jacob was a God-fearing man, but he also battled, as we do, self-centeredness. Letting Benjamin go was the last straw because he was his beloved Rachel's only remaining son. There isn't a single one of us, I'm sure, who can accusingly point a finger at him for hanging onto his youngest son so determinedly. It is perfectly natural. We all have our Benjamins in one form or another—people, things, or plans that we hang onto for dear life, even though we are perfectly miserable in doing so. When we do, we hinder God from fulfilling His purposes in our lives, the plans He had for us since the foundation of the world.

There is, however, one thought that should help us to be willing to say, as Jacob did, "If I am bereaved, I am bereaved." That is to think of the pleasure Jacob would have missed had he not done so. If we imagine Jacob's stepping out of the wagon and into the arms of Joseph, that should help us endure until we, too, see our dreams fulfilled. Thinking how happy we will be to see with our own eyes and to hear with our own ears all the glory of our "Joseph," when we leave our wagons behind. Nothing can light a candle to the celebration and thrill of that glorious day. Why, says Paul, "the sufferings of this present time are not worthy to be compared with the glory which shall be revealed in us" (Rom. 8:18). We will gladly join with the heavenly hosts in expressing our joy, "*...saying with a loud voice, Worthy is the Lamb that was slain to receive power, and riches, and wisdom, and strength, and honor, and glory, and blessing*" (Rev. 5:12).

20
IN IT TOGETHER

"Remember the word unto Thy servant, upon which Thou hast caused me to hope. This is my comfort in my affliction: for Thy word hath quickened me."
PSALM 119:49-50

The day I met with the people who were shouldering the responsibility for the Gumma Machi assembly is a day I shall not soon forget. They had assured me it was for the purpose of fellowship and that it would be an informal gathering. There was no way I could prepare for the personal questions they asked, so I was taken by surprise. Many of those present had been led to the Lord in one of Gifford's Bible classes during their high school years. Now, twenty-some years later they were leaders themselves and there was a common desire to know the secret to abiding faithfully to the end of life, as Gifford had. They asked me about his personal life and what my impressions were of him as a person. As they said, I had lived with him daily.

They had seen his life; but that was not their question. They saw his energy, his directiveness, his urgency in preaching the gospel. They wanted to know where his joy, his untiring love, his endurance, faith, and zeal came from. I could only share ideas that came as I picked my way back through our thirty-one years together.

The first and foremost thought that came to mind was his sensitiveness to sin. The only tears I ever saw him shed were in prayers of confession to the Lord for sin. Even as a child he understood the ugliness of sin in a unique way. He knew he did not deserve to live, much less to live to serve God. He never lost the wonder that came the night he confessed Christ, not only as his Saviour, but as his Lord. He often included in his testimony how that, on his way home that night, he felt like he was walking on air.

He was a man with a purpose for living. He had one desire and that was to live for Christ. He was a man of prayer. His day started with prayer and ended with prayer and had a great deal of prayer in between. He prayed before he left the bedroom in the morning, he prayed with me, he prayed with each person he counseled, and he prayed in groups.

The whole day I was at Gumma Machi, a vision of a group of seven men flashed repeatedly before me. I recalled these young men huddled together around a small kerosene stove trying to at least keep their hands warm. The little stove was the sole source of heart in the cold chapel. For years, I had a snapshot of the group, but have long since lost it. I tried to replace it with a current picture of the seven all together, but it was impossible as they were scattered throughout the area, each in his field of service. I thank God they are all going on with the Lord and are being used by Him.

These seven young men, a special gift from God, represented the core of the Lord's work. Gifford was guiding them in Scripture truths, and they were good kindling wood as the flame caught fire quickly. They committed themselves to staying for prayer together after every meeting held in the chapel, ministry meetings as well as gospel meetings. To me, those prayer meetings seemed to last forever as I waited for Gifford. This went on year in and year out. The little stove was the center of their comfort for body heat, but the real center of their little prayer group was Christ—Immanuel, "God with us." He was their source for spiritual warmth.

Gifford was a man with a message. That message was

100

Christ. I overheard a young man ask him if he ever got tired of talking about the Lord, and his ready answer was, "No." Then he added, "When you can give me a better subject to talk about, I'll change." That challenge was never met. One of the first questions he asked in personal conversations was what the person's motive for living was. He wanted to know what his goal in life was. He could not understand existing in life without an aim.

His focus was worship. The more he saw his unworthiness, the more he appreciated Christ's worthiness, and vice versa. Even as a high school student, he soon recognized the authority of the Bible. He wanted to worship Christ in spirit and in truth. When establishing a foundation for a local church, he sought to follow the pattern for the church given to us by the Holy Spirit through Paul. As Head of His church—the church Christ loved and gave His life for—he knew that He must have the pre-eminence. To Gifford, the truth that man's glory must be covered as a reminder that Christ only deserved the glory was a precious truth. To him these instructions were not optional.

Without doubt, Gifford had the gift of evangelism, especially one-on-one, but that was second to worship as far as he was concerned. He preached the gospel in the United States, China, Taiwan, Korea, and Japan. He preached to gas station attendants, school boys as they sat on mountainsides painting the scenery, on buses and trains, in parks, in dental and doctor's offices, from the platform, and in Bible classes. And he always did it with a big smile! However, he felt that evangelism was only half of Christ's command, so he was constantly teaching the young men everywhere they went together. He seldom went alone; he took a team with him whenever he could. He taught them as they drove, he taught them around the dining room table, he taught them at camp, and on picnics.

It was a thrill of my lifetime to see the eager faces before me that day and to recall all these details in answer to their many questions. That evening I went to bed with a great feeling of gratitude for having been chosen to be a helpmeet to Gifford. I am so thankful that he never let me hinder him or become distracted from fulfilling the special commission the Lord gave him as His servant.

Ah, but I didn't always feel gratitude for my role as helpmeet. We were going through a time in the work of the Lord in Takasaki when the Lord was blessing the daily Bible classes in an unbelievable way. The young people were responding. Every day after the classes, Gifford would bring a car full of students home with him. These young people filled our living room and took turns to receive counsel from him, each with his own questions. There were many converted during that short time who are still going on well with the Lord and are the leaders in the churches today. But I was going through a time of real testing.

Gifford was seeing the blessing, not me. I was in the kitchen preparing dinner for anywhere from five to fifteen (on one special occasion it was twenty-five), but usually five to eight. One afternoon I was having a bad day and feeling extremely sorry for myself. I kept repeating to myself the unanswered question, What am I doing here in Japan, anyway? All I ever do is feed people and write letters.

Believe me, by the time dinner was served, I was not fit to live with—absolutely consumed with self-pity. Well, we got through it. I sang with the rest, read the Bible with the rest after the meal, and even went to the evening meeting with them, but when I came home to a dirty, messy kitchen, my mood was anything but virtuous.

After I got things cleaned up, Gifford was still not home; he was at the chapel, praying with the seven young men who had agreed to pray together after every meeting. Before we bought a second car—so I didn't have to wait to ride home with him— I had seen the joy those men had together. I was envious. And that night I was furious. I was home alone—working, working in the kitchen! He was having all the fun! This wasn't what missionary life was supposed to be—or was it?

I knew in my heart that I could not go on in this state of mind. Something had to happen. So I sat down by the little kerosene stove, took my Bible in hand, and tried to soothe my conscience. The portion was Psalm 68. When I came to verses 11-13, I read the following:

> *The Lord gave the word: great was the company of those that published it. Kings of armies did flee apace: and she that tarried at home divided the spoil. Though ye have lien among the pots, yet shall ye be as the wings of a dove covered with silver, and her feathers with yellow gold.*

The psalm seems to be written with the story of Barak and Deborah's victory over Sisera (Jud. 4 & 5) in mind. (See especially vv. 17-18 with a direct quotation from their victory duet in Jud. 5.) And though Barak led the victorious troops into battle (like my Gifford), Jael working in her tent shared in the victory. In fact, she killed the commander-in-chief himself!

The Spirit of God gripped my attention that night, and these words fairly leapt out of the page: "She that tarried at home divided the spoil. Though ye have lien among the pots, yet..." The Lord Himself seemed to say, "Madge, you're not sharing in all the thrill right now, but don't give up, You'll share in the spoil in your day."

It was as if the Lord had written that scripture just for me. It couldn't have been any clearer. They have often repeated their message since that time. God is not limited nor does He always seem to be fair in His job assignments, but joy in His service is equally available to all, and He will be more than fair when the spoils are divided at the judgment seat of Christ.

21
ONE STRUGGLE AFTER ANOTHER

"And his inward affection is more abundant toward you, while he
remembereth the obedience of you all…"
2 CORINTHIANS 7:15

Everyone who believes on the Lord Jesus Christ is an object of God's matchless mercy, but some of us are "vessels of mercy" in a special sense (Rom. 9:23). Paul himself claimed the Lord would use him as special evidence of the saving power of God. If God could save a murderer of Christians like Saul of Tarsus, no one need despair or give up praying for some difficult unbelieving friend or relative.

It seems, as well, that God chooses to show His life-changing power through the lives of some individuals to a greater degree than others. One such example is a woman I met not long after returning from furlough. The salesgirl in the bookstore called me one morning because she had a customer that she wanted me to meet. Since only one door separated our home from the shop, I was there in a second.

The woman was one of the most charming women I had ever met. She was vivacious, beautiful, and well dressed. At first I felt intimidated and overpowered by her magnetic personality. I became extremely aware of the inadequacy of my Japanese. However, the intensity of her questions soon put me at ease. She asked simple questions about eternal issues, and I forgot the differences between us as we talked about heaven, hell, and the preparation for life after death.

It was evident that her heart was prepared to hear the gospel. She knew she needed the Lord, and she wanted to be saved. I had met many people who were interested in spiritual things, but seldom had I met such a searching heart. At first I thought she might have an ulterior motive. I wondered what it *really* was that brought her into a Christian bookstore. Her desire seemed too good to be true. After talking together for quite some time, however, there was no question about her sincerity. She was seeking the truth about her soul and about life in general.

I prayed silently the whole time we talked, and I felt drawn to this gifted woman. The last thing she asked me before she left was if I had a Bible class for people who knew nothing about the teachings of Christ. I had been in the States for nine months after Gifford passed away, and before that I had been nursing him, so I had nothing in the way of Bible studies to offer her. However, the Lord prompted me to tell her as she was leaving that if she would come the following Friday morning, we could study the Bible together.

She came. We opened the Word together and she, with the Bible she had just purchased that week, kept the conversation going with one question after another. Somewhere in her childhood she had contact with Christian people and had been impressed with their lifestyle and their bright hope for eternal life. We decided that first week to study the Gospel of John together. The first few times she came alone, but it wasn't long before she was bringing some of her friends with her, so it turned into a weekly Bible study with an emphasis on the gospel. For refreshments she always brought the most exotic dainties that she had made herself.

In the meantime, she invited me to visit in her home. It was a beautiful home, well fitted for the position her husband held as the president of a large steel factory in Takasaki. Her luxury and affluence was quite a contrast to that of mine in entertaining the students whom Gifford had brought into our home daily from his Bible classes. But in spite of the differences, a strong and close friendship soon developed.

During the first few months I sensed nothing in her conversation that indicated any problems in her life, but as time went on, she opened up her heart to me after the others had left for their homes. She told me that her husband had made some bad choices in business and that his company's finances were being investigated. Each week as we sat in the study at the "kotatsu" (a low table with cushions on the floor) she shared more and more. It was there that she bared her real fears and emotions. She admitted that they were in trouble, big trouble. One morning she prayed with me and clearly invited Christ into her life.

Underneath her happy exterior she was carrying a sad, confused, and frightened heart. It was not too long after that when the true situation could be covered up no longer. The newspaper blared the news that her husband and the company had declared bankruptcy. They spared no details. The publicity was a disgrace to both their families, but especially hers. It brought a new struggle for her because her family insisted that she divorce her husband, take back her maiden name, and begin a new life of her own in order to save them from disgrace.

She immediately came to me for advice. We searched the Scriptures together and she soon agreed there was no reason for divorce in her case. While she understood how her family felt, she now believed the Bible to be the final authority in her life. She made the choice to obey it's teaching in every way she possibly could, and this included staying with her husband She knew her husband was at fault, but she felt she should stay to help him find a solution to his problems. Greater yet, she now longed for his salvation. When she told her family about her decision, they were understandably very angry and avoided her.

Her husband was grateful for her love and loyalty, so he

tried in every way possible to please her. About that time, Billy Graham came to Tokyo again. Her husband was one of the first to sign up to ride in one of the chartered buses to the Crusade. He had not consented to attend any of the regular meetings at the chapel, so we were overjoyed that he was at least willing to go to Tokyo to hear Billy Graham. He was so impressed by what he heard that night that he decided to stay in Tokyo with his parents and attend the Sunday afternoon service as well. He went forward for counseling following the message. If he wasn't saved that day, it certainly was the beginning of the soul-work that led to his conversion. His was a clear, sincere confession of faith which later proved to be real.

As new believers, this couple's hearts were knit together as never before. They began reading and praying together. This fortified them for the battle which lay ahead of them. She had passed an important milestone in deciding to stay with him, but this next one he would share with her. Together they saw their house sold, their furniture repossessed; they saw their friends disappear, their families avoid them, and they faced unbelievable humility in reading all these details in the daily newspaper. Through all these unfortunate circumstances, they found support and love, as they never imagined, from the believers in the church. The Christians stood behind them as their new-found family. Everyone was praying for their need for a roof over their head and a job for him.

In answer to those prayers, the husband's parents offered the family of four a couple of rooms in which to live, but that meant a move to the Tokyo area. This was not only disappointing to us in Takasaki, but we were worried about seeing such new believers have to move out on their own, especially in living with his unsaved family. We felt they needed us for a little while longer in order to survive the disgrace of the bankruptcy, the grief of losing all their earthly possessions, and of his being out of work.

As usual, our worries were unfounded. The Lord was (at

least) one step ahead of us. There was a fine assembly in the neighborhood where they were going to live. They soon found support and spiritual help from the believers. Besides this, they had each other in a fresh love they had not known possible before. It was a good thing, too, for another struggle lay ahead, equally as difficult as those already endured.

No sooner had they settled in with his parents, than a new trial came their way. At issue was their involvement with the family shrine. They were completely dependent on his parents until he could find employment. His parents made it clear that they were expected to join in the rituals because they were a part of the home. This is a perfectly normal expectation. The suggestions and nagging thoughts that perhaps their whole reversal of circumstances was a type of punishment by the ancestors was not surprising. The battle within raged fiercely and persistently.

Once more the wife came to me for advice and prayer support. Once again we sat in the study, but this time her face was as dark and troubled as a thundercloud. The atmosphere was so thick one could cut it with a knife. I could well imagine what was going through her mind as I suggested reading Hebrews 11:24-27 together.

> *By faith Moses, when he was come to years, refused to be called the son of Pharaoh's daughter; choosing rather to suffer affliction with the people of God, than to enjoy the pleasures of sin for a season; esteeming the reproach of Christ greater riches than the treasures in Egypt; for he had respect unto the reward.*

The whole time we were talking, I was well aware that I was on one side of the table and she was on the other. She was the one who faced eviction if she didn't comply with the family's wishes, not me. At the same time, I had to be faithful to what I believed God was teaching through this passage.

We talked of the struggle that Moses was facing at that time. Pharaoh's daughter had taken him in as a baby and had raised him as her own son. To the world surrounding Moses this was unforgivable ingratitude to turn his back on her. This same feeling of loyalty is inbred in the Japanese, so I doubted that Moses' struggle was any more acute than hers was at that moment. I felt that there was no more that should be said at that moment lest she feel pressured, so I left the room. The truth of the matter was, I had a few issues of compromise I had to settle for myself. I went into the next room to pray and sort out things. I prayed that both of us could have a clear glimpse of the reward awaiting us, as Moses had.

After what seemed like an eternity, I joined her again. I just sat with her for a few minutes. I could sense the battle of the will that was taking place. I was praying that her obligation to Christ would win out over obligations to the family, when all of a sudden her face brightened. She flashed one of the brightest smiles I had seen yet. I knew the decision had been made in the right direction. The sparkle was back in her eye as she told me she was going back to share these thoughts with her husband.

It was with much trepidation that I walked her to the bus stop. I saw her off with a silent prayer for the strength she was going to need. I waited with bated breath until she called to let me know the results of the discussion. Amazingly, it wasn't the problem all of us had thought it might be. The parents respected their convictions and accepted their decision.

They didn't have to stay in that home very long because he soon found a good job. This enabled them to rent a small apartment and be their own family again. God has honored their decision and has blessed their household.

But the best is yet to come. God has promised that the sufferings of this life are not worthy to be compared to the glory which shall be revealed in them. What an exchange of loss for gain when our Saviour give His "Well done!" for any willingness on our part to relinquish the treasures of this life in obedience to His Word.

22
PARENTING

"And thou shalt remember all the way which the Lord thy God led thee...to humble thee, and to prove thee, to know what was in thine heart, whether thou wouldest keep His commandments, or no."
DEUTERONOMY 8:2

I am often asked for tips on parenting. As a result, I have given considerable thought to the subject. I certainly am not an authority on the subject, but I have learned from both positive and negative experiences in my own life. I have lived long enough to have watched other parents and their families, and have learned from them, too. On that basis, may I share some of my thoughts on the issue of parenting? Over the years the Lord has assured me repeatedly that my failures are not final. He is perfectly capable of rectifying my shortcomings, But I would be pleased if I thought some young mother would be spared similar negative experiences which the Lord has found necessary to bring me through.

If we use God as our role model, we will gain a few good ideas on parenting. One of the first lessons to teach our children is, as I see it, the first lesson God taught Adam and Eve: that actions have consequences. He promised consequences for disobedience. After Adam and Eve disobeyed Him, He gave consequences, very severe consequences. If you don't agree, just think about it the next time you wipe perspiration from your brow as a result of weeding your garden.

The very fact that you may be one of those who has asked

questions about parenting, proves that you have experienced firsthand the pains of childbirth as a result of Eve's share in the fall. Children who are constantly shielded from reaping consequences soon learn to think they can "get away with it," a sure way to reap a bumper crop of sorrow.

When Adam and Eve sinned, God made it so they had to keep busy. There is great wisdom in that consequence planned by God. Imagine how much trouble the human race would get into if we didn't have to work eight hours a day!

Many emotional problems begin when a child has too much time to think his or her own thoughts. When they think their own thoughts and go their own way, their thinking soon becomes warped. To prevent this, God said that man was to work for a living, keeping his mind occupied with things other than himself.

That principle should begin in childhood. Laziness is a life-long enemy of the human race. I might add that, as any woman who is responsible for the care of children knows, children certainly keep our minds off ourselves!

Children should learn early to share the ministry of care giving as well. We might do well to take note that God did not explain *why* they were to obey. When they disobeyed, He gave consequences immediately, and let them learn as they suffered from them.

Remember His example when one of your children has a tantrum and deliberately breaks a favorite toy. Explain that he or she no longer has that toy as a consequence of his or her own actions. Our children need to know that God always forgives any sin when we are sorry. However, He doesn't erase the consequences of our actions. In His grace, He often gives us a poor crop when we sow wild oats, but our children should learn early in life that if we ignore the rules of health, we are likely to suffer physical problems; we can't blame God when we do. It is the same with emotional and spiritual problems. We, as parents, should be aware that more than one child has had to enter the hospital to have his or her stomach pumped out because poison was eaten in innocence. Unfortunately, there is no hospital that can pump out spiritual or emotional poison before it does its damage.

In addition to developing their awareness of consequences, we would do well to consider how we can help our children build character. Character building is done by creating good daily habits. And it is done by teaching honesty.

Consider another of God's choice children—Abraham. He is known as a man of great faith and the father of the Jewish nation. In the Scriptures, I see that God was very diligent in His training of Abraham's character, and that He never stopped training him. He began when he was a young man.

God worked on his inclination toward deceit, causing Abraham to be humbled by the consequence of a half-truth. He was rebuked by a Gentile and sent on his way as the result of a lie. Abraham was God's beloved child, but He did not shield him from the embarrassing truth that Sarah was not really his full sister. I was often tempted to shield my children because I was worried that God would lose face in disgrace. God doesn't worry about that. God is much more concerned about holiness in the lives of His children. He wants the power of strong character in His family.

Going back to God as our role model again, we see Him training Joseph in adapting to disappointments in life. Joseph had to learn early that life is not always fair, nor is it just. He learned to respond in a godly way to some very severe trials and injustice. Joseph was fully aware that the Lord was with him in all these adverse circumstances. I believe it was knowing that God was with him that gave him the ability to adjust to every unpleasant situation in which he found himself. Our children will be strong Christians if they believe that God is faithful and able to give them strength for every temptation. It will make them seek the way of escape that He promises.

Another example of God's parenting is of King David.

Much of his success in ruling the people of God later was the patience he learned in having to wait so long for the promises of God to be fulfilled. Seldom does a person qualify to rule others if he has not learned to *be* ruled. It was many years from the time he was anointed to be king of Israel until the actual day of his coronation. During that time, God taught him valuable lessons through the need for patience.

Jude rehearses for us the lessons that Enoch must have learned in his family. He gives us the message Enoch passed on of warnings of judgment against such common sins as: murmuring, grumbling, walking after their own lusts (doing their own thing), bragging, seeking the admiration of men, etc. May our children learn that these common sins are not to be found within our walls. Surely the one great desire of every Christian parent is that their children learn to walk with God as Enoch did.

Mary must have learned acceptance as a child because she was still a very young woman when an angel approached her with a very troubling announcement. It was news that would put her in a bad light with friends and family unless they, too, would believe the message. She didn't need much time to quietly agree in her heart, *"...Be it unto me according to Thy word."* The earlier our children can learn this lesson in acceptance, the better it will be for them, and us.

Blessed is the parent who learns, while their children are still very young, to walk before them in the fear of the Lord. The Lord is adamant that it is the fear of Him that gives wisdom. We certainly want our children to be wise people. This is only done through our walking with the Lord ourselves and showing them by our example.

By using God our Father as our example, we learn the balance of walking before Him in fear and in gentleness and goodness, realizing ourselves that *"...the wrath of man worketh not the righteousness of God"* (Jas. 1:20).

114

23
PRECIOUS PROMISES PROVEN

*"And they remembered that God was their rock,
and the high God their redeemer.*
PSALM 78:35

We all know the hurt of broken promises. I think I was sent to bed without my supper more often as a punishment for breaking promises than for any other offense. In our family, we were repeatedly taught that promises were made to be kept; breaking them was not permitted. Character can be judged by whether we stick to our word or not. Promises are important to God, too.

In Hebrews 11:33-34, God links promises with faith. In this respect, however, He emphasizes our need to believe the promises *He* makes rather than the importance of keeping the promises we make to others.

...Who through faith subdued kingdoms, wrought righteousness, obtained promises, *stopped the mouths of lions, quenched the violence of fire, escaped the edge of the sword, out of weakness were made strong, waxed valiant in fight, turned to flight the armies of the aliens.*

In the midst of all these heroic acts is the one we might overlook: obtained promises! God is pleased when we express our faith in Him by standing on the promises He makes to us. The Lord has always put a special premium on His people's taking Him at His Word. God is actually grieved when we doubt what He says. He desires that we have enough faith in Him to believe He will accomplish His promises. He wants us to trust Him for who He is. Doubting what He says is the same as doubting Him, for a person is as good as his word. Our trust puts His character at stake.

The eyes of the world see nothing spectacular about holding tenaciously on to what one believes. In fact, thy often label it as stubbornness or stupidity, but God places great value on this act of faith. He loves it when I'm willing to stake my life on what He says in His Word. When discussing this recently, I was asked if I'd proven any of God's promises to be true for myself. I was caught off guard and was hard pressed to single out any one promise. But when they came to mind, first one came, then another, and another. Allow me to share a few.

Umpteen years ago, I read a Bible promise at a time I was having a related problem. It is a promise that Christ Himself gave in Matthew 6:25-33,

> *Take no thought for your life...nor yet for your body, what ye shall put on...Seek ye first the kingdom of God and His righteousness and all these things shall be added unto you.*

My problem was self-inflicted, but it was urgent nonetheless. I had gained weight and literally had nothing suitable in my closet that fit. I was feeling so low that I needed a ladder to climb up to the bottom. I managed to find something for everyday wear, but I'd been asked to walk down the aisle with the bride at her wedding. I could hardly sneak in the back door unnoticed!

I had returned from shopping and had found nothing in the entire city of Takasaki. In those days, very few stores sold western-style, ready-made goods, and ones they did sell were made for petite Japanese ladies. I was discouraged. Furthermore, I felt very guilty for having let my weight creep up as it had, but that didn't help. The wedding was the following week. So I did what a few other women do under such circumstances. I cried, and had my own little pity party. Then an incident that I'd had when I was a schoolgirl, came to mind.

I had gone to my earthly father for shoes, but there was no money available. It was during the Depression. He had three dollars in his pocket, earmarked to buy food for the weekend. So I did what was normal in our home; I went to my heavenly Father. As Dad walked down the hallway, he heard my earnest prayer and knew that the faith of a child was at stake. When I came out of the room, he suggested we go to town together. As you've guessed, I got my shoes. Later that day, an envelope was left in our mailbox, benefactor unknown, with our food money. Was it a coincidence? No! Was it a promise kept? Yes! (See Phil. 4:19).

With this memorial in mind, I decided to pray as I had so many years before. But first I opened my Bible to find something with which to strengthen my faith. I turned to the above verses. It seemed as if the Lord was teasing me. My situation looked so hopeless and impossible. I had no Dad to help me out this time. But I claimed those words for myself.

I had quoted them dozens of times to others, but this time was different. They suddenly had teeth in them. The Lord seemed to ask me if I was ready to try them out as an adult. I agreed to trust Him because at that stage, if the Lord didn't step in, I was sunk. With no patterns on hand, I could not sew up something.

In only a matter of minutes, I remembered one of the two-piece dresses I had looked at while shopping. Both the blouse and the skirt had front pleats, so if I took the pleats out, the dress might fit. I got back into the car and went to the store once more. After looking it over carefully, I knew it could be done. And it was done. After a good press, it looked as if it had been styled that way from the beginning. The following week, I walked my beautiful bride down the aisle. I was pleased with what the Lord and I had done together.

The story did not end that day, however. It continues to this day. In fact, if you saw my closets today, you would agree that I face the opposite question: Which one do I pick?

A second promise that came to mind occurred when I was getting ready to visit Japan in 1992 for the dedication of the new camp grounds. I walked into my bedroom to find a puddle of rainwater on top of my computer! I looked up just as a drop formed in a tiny crack in the ceiling and dropped with a plop into the puddle. I can't leave for Japan with a leaky roof, I thought. Simultaneously Isaiah 54:5 popped into my mind.

For thy maker is thine husband: The Lord of hosts is His name.

I recognized the verse as one I have used with widows many times, but this time it came with fresh meaning for me. I knew that if Gifford were living, I would have no trouble leaving for Japan because he would be there to fix things. He always looked after those details for me, so I hadn't worried about anything.

I wrestled with my problem for a time, but that evening I attended a small group prayer meeting and mentioned this need for prayer. A dear brother there said that he had a friend who repaired roofs, and that he would contact him. He also promised to oversee the job for me. I had perfect peace, believing that my Maker was doing what my husband had done many times in hiring someone to do the job for Him. I left for Japan very relieved as I claimed the promise in Psalm 146:9,

The Lord…relieveth the fatherless and widow.

A third promise that came to mind happened within days after Gifford went to be with the Lord. Even though he had been very sick, his mind was clear, and he had still been able to advise me on all the details of running our home—the car, income taxes, and the like. One thing he had forgotten to prepare me for, however, was the yearly car inspection. The sticker on the windshield would expire within days, and I had no idea how to go about having it renewed.

As ridiculous as this problem may seem to the normal thinking person, it was no small matter to me. Within minutes my molehill grew to mountain size. With all the other formalities that had to be attended to, this was the last straw. I walked into the study where his bed had been for the previous six months, and it looked so empty and forbidding. I wanted so badly to ask him just one more "how to" question, but he wasn't there. To fill out application forms is one thing in English, but the thoughts of filling out forms in Japanese seemed too much.

At that moment, Matthew 12:42 flashed before me:

Behold a greater than Solomon is here.

It was as if the Lord was saying, "Madge, I'm still here; isn't that enough?" My heart answered honestly, "No, Lord," but He soon reminded me that He was wiser and greater than either Solomon or Gifford. He would inform me of anything I needed to know. He literally did that for me by prompting me to look through Gifford's files for help. I soon found papers I felt would be useful, and with these papers in hand I took off. Actually I found the officials most helpful and they filled out the application forms. As I drove home, looking to my heavenly Father who was substituting as my husband, I felt like a child who had discovered he had grown an inch taller. I rested assured that He would take responsibility for me regarding clothing, roofs, wisdom, or even car inspection stickers.

Putting these events down on paper has reminded me that God's promises are true for myself when I take Him at His word.

24
PROMISES AND MORE PROMISES

"O give thanks unto the Lord; for He is good: for His mercy endureth for ever...Who remembered us in our low estate: for His mercy endureth for ever: and hath redeemed us from our enemies: for His mercy endureth for ever."
Psalm 136:1, 23-24

A lot of people have walked out of my life. Some left me in the lurch. Some didn't need my friendship any longer. Some left because circumstances changed and distance caused a loss of contact. But many more of those who have been closest to me left through death.

Thank God, I never need to worry about my Closest Friend ever leaving me for any reason. Why am I so confident? He promised me He wouldn't. In Hebrews 13:5-6, Christ has assured me that He will never leave me. More than once this thought has comforted me greatly:

Let your manner of life be without covetousness, and be content with such things as ye have: for He hath said, I will never leave thee, nor forsake thee, so that we may boldly say, The Lord is my helper, and I will not fear what man shall do unto me.

I can be content and never be afraid because Christ plainly has said that He will never forsake me. He will never leave me in the lurch. He will never tire of my friendship. Distance never even enters into the picture because He is constantly within. He will never die because He did it once as a sacrifice for my sin, but then arose and lives forever in the power of an endless life.

Why, then, should I ever be afraid? As a child, I remember having nightmares which, for some strange reason, used to end with a severe nosebleed. My father used to come and sit on the bed after Mom got the nosebleed stopped, and he just sat there. It was such a comfort to me that, before I knew it, it was morning.

Someone greater than my father is with me at all times. In my childish way of thinking, my father could do anything; but Christ, who has promised never to leave me, is the Lord of the universe. All the power that hurled the universe into existence is right here with me, twenty-four hours a day. I can rest in confidence that He is the ever-present help in every time of need.

Even though I know that God is with me, I have difficulty at times with my emotions because He becomes silent. He just sits there. In Dad's case, he was quiet so that I would go back to sleep. He wanted to get some rest himself. I know that God never has that motive, but I'm sure that He has a motive in His silence, too. I have learned that I do well if I read the context of the promise that I am claiming, either before or after the promise, to see if there might be some qualification or stipulation that I have not noticed that came with the promise. There is often some lesson He wants me to learn through His silence. In the above verse, on the occasion in which I claimed it, I noticed that with His promise to be with me, He asks me to live without covetousness and to be content with whatever lot in life He had already given me.

I soon recognized the fact that the little monster, covetousness, had come in and caused ungratefulness. Once he was in, discontentment wormed his way in to ruin my fellowship with the Lord. I believe this is Paul's reason for referring to covetousness as idolatry. Unfaithfulness and ingratitude often cause my Lord to be silent. The Lord admits to being a jealous

God. He is jealous of my affection, and when He sees that there are other things and people I am coveting, He is grieved. When He is grieved, He becomes silent.

Other culprits that cause a lack of harmony and fellowship with my Lord are: my unkindness, anger, bitterness, and especially unforgiveness, toward one of His other children. God loves all His children, and when I have a difference with one of them, He grieves and becomes quiet. He treats me like that because He knows we can only live in happiness as a family when we are in harmony with Him and with His children.

It's for my good that He disciplines me through silence. How can He give me what I want when I am a disobedient daughter? It just doesn't work. I've found that there's no hope of my being filled with the Spirit (Eph. 5:18) as long as I'm grieving His Spirit by my sinful attitude toward one of His children (Eph. 4:30-31). It's impossible for my heart to be filled with His singing when it's filled with such thoughts as are mentioned there. The two are incompatible.

At other times, when He has become silent, I have become aware that I had failed to take time for fellowship with Him in prayer. As a result, I have assumed His responsibility by taking it on myself to try to work things out. This attitude also displeases Him. At still other times, He becomes silent for no apparent reason at all. I don't have to probe to find His reason; I just accept it and go on by faith from there.

One afternoon, following a conversation with an airline agent, I had an interesting thought on prayer. I had called to make a reservation for a trip to Chicago. All I did was give her my last name and she immediately asked, "Madge, do you still live on Clarkson?" I was taken by surprise that she had this information in a split second. She had pushed a button on her computer, and my address and a lot of other data came up on her screen. She even knew how many travel miles I had collected. God certainly is no less efficient. Computers are no marvel to Him. This encouraged me in intercessory prayer as well. He also keeps data on the person for whom I'm praying. He knows their current needs, their struggles, their doubts, and the opposition they may be facing.

Getting back to the thought of claiming and standing on God's promises, let's go back to the offer which seems to be one of my favorites, John 7:37-38:

> ...If any man thirst, let him come unto Me, and drink. He that believeth on Me, as the scripture hath said, out of his heart shall flow rivers of living water.

The moment I feel thirsty from spiritual dehydration, if I go directly to Him and ask for a drink, He gives me a refreshing supply. But if I merely ask Him for whatever it is I want at the moment, I often don't feel refreshed. The answer is that, although I have come, I haven't received from Him. We've all heard many times that we can lead a horse to water, but we can't make him drink. This is true of people, too. The drinking is voluntary. If I don't meet His qualifications that accompany His promise, the weakness caused by my thirst will continue and I will soon be accusing Him of silence. A tragic outcome of not drinking is that there is no water to gush out to others.

The same principle is true as found in Christ's promise in John 8:12:

> ...I am the light of the world; he that followeth Me shall not walk in darkness, but shall have the light of life.

If I wake up in the morning in a dark mood, confused, and feel that Christ is not very real, it helps me to claim this promise. I must believe that He is still the Light of the World. My problem is that I've decided to go in a different direction all together. If we walk in the light, John tells us in his first epistle, then we have fellowship with Him.

If someone has hurt my feelings, if my pride has been hurt, my rights have been infringed upon, or I've lost my joy in the Lord, a promise which has often helped me is Isaiah 29:19:

The meek also shall increase their joy in the Lord, and the poor among men shall rejoice in the Holy One of Israel.

The application is self-explanatory.

One more promise which has helped me keep my sanity and encouraged me to keep my armor on is Isaiah 49:24-25.

Shall the prey be taken from the mighty, or the lawful captive delivered? But thus saith the Lord: Even the captives of the mighty shall be taken away, and the prey of the terrible shall be delivered; for I will contend with him that contendeth with thee, and I will save thy children.

While waiting for the Lord to fulfill this promise in my life and in the lives of others, it has been a comfort to think of Samson's parents. What was it that kept them steady when Samson turned out to be such a rebellious young adult? Before he was born, they asked God how to raise him. I'm sure that when he was a child, they entrusted him to the Lord. I can imagine that, many times, they questioned what they had done wrong. I'm sure there were those around them who were very glad to inform them what it was; but were they not driven to their knees during those formative years seeking guidance from the Lord, and later while they were waiting for the Lord to work in Samson's life? We know from reading Hebrews 11 that the Lord did work in his life by restoring his faith even at the end. The Lord did snatch him as prey from the hands of Satan.

As far as I'm concerned, the promise that tops them all off is found in 2 Corinthians 6:18:

And I...will be a Father unto you, and ye shall be my sons and daughters, saith the LORD ALMIGHTY.

A point that is not to be forgotten is that verse 17 precedes the promises and 7:1 follows:

125

Wherefore, come out from among them, and be ye separate, saith the Lord, and touch not the unclean thing; and I will receive you. Having, therefore, these promises, dearly beloved, let us cleanse ourselves from all filthiness of the flesh and spirit, perfecting holiness in the fear of God.

As shameful as it is to say this, familiarity even with such great promises as these can cause them to lose their punch. But knowing my weakness, He understands, and I ask Him for a new fresh one. The old ones, however, keep coming back with invigorating freshness, too. One example is Jeremiah 29:11-14:

For I know the thoughts that I think toward you, saith the Lord, thoughts of peace, and not of evil, to give you an expected end…ye shall seek Me, and find Me, when ye shall search for Me with all your heart.

I do well to remind myself every now and then that He says that His thoughts are of grace. He doesn't say that He'll conform His thoughts to fit mine, but He does say that what He has planned is to keep us in His peace.

Sometimes we have to wait a long time to see the promise fulfilled (as Samson's parents did) but let's not grieve Him with our impatience. His promises are well worth waiting for! He will not disappoint us!

25
RECOGNIZING MINISTRY OPPORTUNITIES

"Wherefore, he saith, Awake thou that sleepest, and arise from the dead, and Christ shall give thee light. See, then, that ye walk circumspectly, not as fools, but as wise, redeeming the time, because the days are evil. Wherefore be ye not unwise but understanding what the will of the Lord is."
EPHESIANS 5:14-17

God is always busy and involved in the lives of the people He created. The amazing thing is, He invites us to join Him.

I have often wondered why God chooses to use ordinary people like you and me, when it seems He can just as easily send His angels down. Although angels would probably do a much better job, He chooses to use us so that He can reveal His power through us. In the same way that the cross is the memorial of God's love and power for redemption, it is also the monument of His power to work in the lives of His saints. I find it terrifically encouraging to know that the Lord had me in mind for a ministry before the foundations of the world. That thought alone gives me the strength and desire to seek out and find that ministry.

Women of any age have a special ministry in the form of role models, and it is especially important for young women to have older women to look up to. I, for example, had an unusually good role model early in my married life. She was seventy when I met her, and she continued to be an inspiration to me for twenty-five years.

The last time I visited her, she told me how happy she was to still be able to peel potatoes for her daughter when she entertained. This statement exemplified her whole life. The very first time I saw her, she invited us for Sunday dinner and invited me to pray with her the following Tuesday morning. Hers was a wide ministry for the Lord. She soon had me visiting shut-ins with her. She sent out hundreds of boxes of used clothing for missionaries of which I was often the recipient. The one word that comes to mind when I think of her is "doer." She was always busy doing something for the Lord; still peeling potatoes at age 95.

I had another role model when I was in my teens. This dear sister was a model in the ministry of suffering. Her husband was in a mental institution so she was left alone to raise nine children. But she never let the subject come into a conversation. She taught a class of girls on Tuesday night. She taught us how to knit, crochet, sew, and bake. Most important, she taught us how to love, how to trust the Lord to supply food for the table, how to teach our children wisdom and how to mature gracefully in the Lord without self-pity. She also was a "doer" with boundless energy.

In contrast to these more active sisters is the example of a quiet homemaker who encouraged us throughout our missionary life by her faithful letters. She wrote about such mundane things as tomatoes in her garden; but how we missed her letters when she got sick and had to stop for a time. She was a true prayer warrior who faithfully served the Lord. She would often ask about those we had written about in our earlier letters. She asked how their problems were solved and how they were doing.

By far, the woman who influenced my life the most as a lifelong role model was my quiet, Spirit-filled mother. For close to seventy years she walked before me with confidence in the Lord. I saw the difference of life before and after she was saved. She often reminded me what my life could have been had she not trusted Christ. I saw her pray her way through just about every type of problem there was. I saw her quiet faith in God.

There are always opportunities for ministry in the Body of Christ, the local church. Christ is always at work building His Church. It is the object of His love, so much so that He was willing to lay down His life for it. Since we should love it the way He does, it shouldn't be hard for us to find ways to serve the church. We, like Phoebe, can all be servants of the church.

The first suggestion I have for ministry within the local church is a praying ministry, and there isn't one sister in the Lord who can't claim this ministry. We are encouraged to pray one for another. We are commanded to pray for all the saints. Prayer takes time and is hard work.

The first time I attended a prayer meeting in the assembly in which I now fellowship, I sat next to a woman who made me feel perfectly at home by flashing me a big smile. After the service, we struck up a conversation and she invited me to her home to pray with her. Our prayers together began a friendship that was strengthened with each weekly visit I made. One wonderful feature of prayer is that there is no gap either in time or distance. We usually stayed close to home in these prayers, but at times the two of us covered the world with our intercession.

The ministry of consolation is always needed in the local church. The Lord told Isaiah to comfort His people, and it is worth noting that Isaiah did so by bringing their thoughts to the Messiah that was to come. In those days the promise of Christ's coming was a hope and a comfort, but no more of a hope than it is today. Jesus is still the answer to the problems of the world, of families, and of individuals. We cannot neglect our responsibilities to bring people to Him. Job's friends sat in silence to show their sympathy for him, but it didn't help much. Then they tried to solve his problem, but that didn't help, either. The only thing that consoled and strengthened

Job was to know God. He needed a fresh encounter with God Himself. We can do nothing better than to bring people under the influence of Christ. The ministry of exhortation is very closely connected to that of consolation for it often goes hand in hand.

Hospitality knows no bounds for ministry. Hospitality is not the same as entertaining, however. Scriptural hospitality as a ministry is always for the purpose of either introducing someone to the Lord, or to encourage them to have a closer walk with Christ by showing that you care. Hospitality doesn't necessarily have to be in one's home; it can be expressed through a cup of coffee or tea almost anywhere. I have often been the recipient of hospitality outside of homes.

Hospitality can include supplying those who are ministering to others by baking a batch of cookies or brownies for them to serve. Many times such people are under time pressures and they would be most grateful if they knew ahead of time that you would be dropping by with a plate of goodies, especially if they know they can depend on you to do so. Don't let them down, however.

Another ministry is to be available for phone calls at any time. Young people often *need* to talk when they *want* to talk, and it helps to hear a cheerful voice at the other end of the line when they are feeling down. Always make time for a short prayer at the end of the conversation. When you see a clouded face on the Lord's Day, ask if the individual would mind if you called. Regardless of the answer, let the person know that she can always cry on your shoulder if she needs to. But don't probe. When she is ready to share her burden, it will come out. As a word of caution, ask the Lord for wisdom to recognize those who only want to take your time and are not really looking for permanent answers from the Lord.

A wide-open field for ministry is that of teaching. Our teaching can never go into retirement. In fact, it is to be the specialty of older sisters. It is good to remember that all teaching is to be preceded by a holy example. We must be serious about eternal issues before we teach others. We must be prudent before we tell others that God requires it. We must be examples of chastity in conversation before we can instruct a younger generation to be pure and modest.

The presence of exchange students in most cities in the United States has opened up a ministry to international students. Students often welcome a conversation in a mall or bus. One of the reasons they are here is to learn English. So if you speak slowly to them, you will more than likely find them responsive. Ask them to have a soda with you, but don't refuse to let the person pay for his or her own beverage, if they express the desire. This is deeply rooted in many of their cultures, especially in those from Asian countries.

Such a simple invitation might open up an opportunity to teach a student the Bible in English. If you find a receptive heart, it can lead to periodically meeting with them in which you may teach them precept upon precept, line upon line. The main thing is not to push the "Western religion" onto them. If the student feels you really care, he or she may bring a friend the next time you meet. Many students have been saved through such a contact with Christians in the United States.

To sum up these thoughts, let me quote what Paul told a believer in Colossians 4:17, *"Take heed to the ministry which thou hast received in the Lord, that thou fulfill it."*

Let us remember that we really are ministering to the Lord when we minister to His children. Let us then remember that He will evaluate our ministry. He will make a memorial to our lives. What words will He choose to engrave upon it? It could hardly be better than His assessment of Enoch: "He pleased God."

26
SALVATION'S MONUMENT

"And their sins and iniquities will I remember no more."
HEBREWS 10:17

It is impossible for me to say just when the capstone to the monument of my salvation was placed, but I know the first stone went down the year I was in kindergarten. I remember the house, the cabinet-type radio, before which I stood and prayed, and even part of the message given. The actual rebirth took place sometime during the next five years. Neither of my parents were saved when I heard that first message, so they could not help in answering my questions. One year after that first spiritual nudge via the radio program, my father was truly born again. One year following that, my mother accepted Christ as her personal Saviour.

I certainly wanted to be saved. I wanted to know the God about whom the message centered, but I don't remember that the preacher mentioned about Christ and His death on the cross. As I try to recollect the event, he did not touch on the need for salvation because of sin. I have no idea why it took so long for me to be assured of my salvation, but I'm thankful that the Lord did not give up on me. The seed planted that first day was well watered in those following years. I recall praying many times with my parents, my Sunday school teachers, and alone, but I have no idea why it took so long.

On the day of my mother's baptism, the Lord again caused a stirring within my heart, and I began to feel conviction of sin for the first time. I was aware that I had lied, I had withheld my offering by putting it in my purse instead of the offering plate—and on top of that, I'd been careless and had soiled and ripped my new Easter dress! I was one miserable girl all day long, but still not miserable enough to be honest in sharing any of this with anyone else—not even the Lord.

However, the Lord had His own ways. For the next few years, I was faced with the reality of death three distinct times. The policeman who directed traffic in front of our school was shot to death. We youngsters loved this man because he not only did it as his duty to serve and protect, he loved us and always had a joke or jolly greeting as he whistled us across the street.

The morning he lost his life he had tried to stop a speeding car. The driver had just robbed the town bank and was escaping. He must have thought the policeman was out for him, so he or his passenger pulled a gun and shot. In the process, one of my classmates was also hit. He lived, but the policeman never recovered. Three friends and I visited his widow and I still remember her as she lay on the couch, ice pack on her aching head, trying to deal with the grief.

Another of my classmates was killed in a sledding accident between Christmas and New Year. She hit a tree and died instantly. It was a glum class that tried to cope with this upon our return to school after vacation.

Then a train ran into the car of our church treasurer and a relative. We were very close to this family; they had visited us just the evening before. Their children were close friends of my brother and me. I was tremendously impacted by the contrast between the two people who died. One, a believer, died in peace. The other, an unsaved relative, died with the words, "It's too late," on his lips. That statement was often repeated during the preaching of the gospel for the next few weeks. I couldn't forget it, though I tried.

In addition to these three incidents, I was obsessed with the story of the kidnapping and death of the famous Lindbergh baby. At that time the papers were full of details. I also listened to every newscast about the case. Death became very real and frightful.

During this time, my father gave a series of Sunday night messages concerning prophecy. He ended every sermon with the thought that Christ was definitely coming soon, that it could well be that very night. Daddy always looked so happy when he spoke of the Lord's return, but it struck fear to my heart. I had no assurance that I would be taken up with Christ. I was terrified of dying, but equally afraid of being left behind alone.

All of these incidents and fears came to a climax one afternoon when I was ten. I returned from school to find our house empty. Mother was the kind of mom who was always there, but this day, as I ran from room to room there was no response to my urgent calls. I ran into their bedroom and found Dad's pants on the floor by the bed. Immediately I knew that Christ had come and I had not been taken with my family (or so I thought)!

In reality, there had been a family emergency. The pants must have slipped from the bed in his hurry. I was hysterical. By the time my parents returned home, one glance at my face and they knew that I was deeply troubled.

Strangely enough, I don't remember the details of our conversation, but I do remember the peace that finally came as a result of it. My parents helped me to see that although I didn't "feel" saved, God had already forgiven my sins. Dad carefully repeated the gospel to me and we prayed again together. Inner peace came when I stopped laboring for the feelings of salvation and simply believed that He had heard my confession and forgiven me. I found that salvation was not all that complicated after all!

I wish I could say that the peace and rest I felt that day lasted ever after, but I must admit that it was a long, stormy battle for me to remain in that state. I experienced a history of ups and downs. I slipped in and out of feeling saved. When I was "up," it was as if a light went on inside and I wondered how I ever had felt so "down" and in the dark. I was always so disappointed when I recognized that I still sinned so often.

To be perfectly truthful, that period extended until after my marriage. It was my husband, Gifford, who helped me see the difference between God's perfect forgiveness and the consequences of sin. If he told me once, he told me a dozen times, "Salvation is a gift and it does not rest on your performance." He reminded me that we do not have to earn our acceptance with God after our salvation any more than we had to earn our salvation in the first place.

In one of these times of discouragement, Gifford merely looked at me and asked, "Why are you so disappointed in yourself? Didn't you know you were a sinner by nature?" He added that we need a Saviour *after* salvation for the same reason we needed to be saved. These truths gave me a new appreciation for Christ and the work He accomplished on the cross for me. My confession did not make my salvation more sure, but it surely improved my fellowship with God because it reminded me of His wonderful grace! It made me grateful for a patient and kind husband, too.

> *Truly our fellowship is with the Father, and with His Son, Jesus Christ...if we walk in the light, as He is in the light, we have fellowship one with another, and the blood of Jesus Christ, His Son, cleanseth (the ever-present cleansing) us from all sin...If we confess our sins, He is faithful and just to forgive us our sins, and to cleanse us from all unrighteousness* (1 Jn. 1:3, 7, 9).

27
TEARS

"Thou tellest [measurest] my wanderings: put Thou my tears into Thy bottle: are they not in Thy book?"
PSALM 56:8

Can you imagine what it would be like to have all of our emotions bottled up inside, without ever having the release made possible through tears? It might be harder for some to imagine than for others. But just thinking about this fact made me realize afresh that God thought of everything when He created us. He even thought of tiny tear ducts.

Men, for some reason, often find tears hard to handle. My dear husband was no exception. After a hard week at camp, I burst into tears one day. For Gifford, my tears were a puzzle he felt he had to solve. For me, it was a release from the pressures of a week of being with teenagers. As he probed, I had a difficult time convincing him that he was in no way the culprit. I was physically exhausted and would simply feel better after a good cry. I was honest when I told him there was no cause that required a remedy, but that I just needed to let out pent-up feelings of strain. I have shed tears for many reasons, real or imaginary, and am thankful that God made it possible to cry.

I remember well the day I received a tape from a friend in the United States labeled *Tears*. Feeling a strong need for comfort at the time, I sat down immediately and listened. That tape was a spiritual marker in my life. It gave me new hope that day, and the thoughts expressed have encouraged me dozens of times since. The tape was based on Psalm 126, and the speaker reminded us that although tears are a part of life, life must go on in spite of them. The Psalmist begins,

When the Lord turned again the captivity of Zion, we were like them that dream.

At the time it was written, the children of Israel were in captivity. They were slaves, so when they were released, it was as if they were walking around in a dream: freedom was just too good to be true. The tears were tears of joy. Although the Old Testament saints were promised physical blessings and help, we find the New Testament often applies these same promises and challenges spiritually. The blessings may differ, but the principles are the same.

The Israelites were captives to real enemies. Theirs was a hard life. They could see and feel the effects of slavery. Today, we are also surrounded by enemies, enemies just as real and even more dangerous than the physical enemies the children of Israel faced. The difference is that we can't see them with our physical eyes even though we know they are there. We are often taken captive by these enemies unaware, and sometimes we become our own enemies as Satan influences us in various ways and brings us into captivity to sin.

The Israelites were taken captive as punishment for straying away from the one, true, living God and for serving false gods. We must admit that we, too, often become the slaves of sin for the same reasons. We become careless in our relationship with God and permit other things to replace Him in our lives. Before we know it, we are imprisoned by fear, anger, bitterness, self-pity, and the like. As soon as we refuse to bring every thought into captivity to Christ, we become captive to our thoughts. When we base daily life on what the world thinks, feels, and does, rather than on what God states and expects, we open the way for the enemy to take us as prey.

Once we forget that the Word of God is the authority and basis for life, we open ourselves to this possibility.

Fear has often been the enemy that has bound me, making me useless to God, myself, or anyone else. It's amazing how little it takes to set off a fresh fear. Real fears, false fears, and imaginary fears all work together to keep me a prisoner. Fear of being falsely or unfairly accused, and fear of sickness, poverty, inadequacy, rejection, and disapproval are just a few of the most common fears I have experienced.

Unresolved problems from my childhood are equally able to imprison me. An unforgiving spirit and worry are classic examples of the enemies of my soul. They keep me from thinking clearly and force me into a state of spiritual paralysis in which I have no freedom to happily serve the Lord.

Repentance toward God and a sincere cry from the heart for help never failed to cause God to set the Israelite captives free. Sometimes it seemed to take forever to be released. I have found the same principle to be effective today. We do an injustice to ourselves and others when we think we can be released from captivity by bettering ourselves by works. There are formulas by the dozens, but the one that works without fail for me has been:

If My people, who are called by My name, shall humble themselves, and pray, and seek My face, and turn from their wicked ways, then will I hear from heaven, and will forgive their sin, and will heal their land (2 Chron. 7:14).

When God begins the healing process, the relief is so great that it is like walking around in a dream. The experience almost defies description. But the Psalmist expressed it well:

Then was our mouth filled with laughter, and our tongue with singing: then said they among the nations, the Lord has done great things for them (v. 2).

When I noticed verse 4, I was encouraged to know that the

Israelites' captivity occurred more than once, so they had to cry out for freedom many times:

Turn again our captivity, O Lord, like the streams in the Negev.

Since this was Israel's history, I don't have to be disappointed if I must cry out repeatedly as well.

Then the Psalmist introduced another subject, that of tears. Often tears of pain follow tears of joy. They had been freed, but the tears did not end. Life had to go on. He indicated that seed had to be sown, and it was often done with tears for one reason or another. Even after experiencing a glorious victory and walking around in such happiness that they thought they were dreaming, they were not permanently freed from sorrow. So the Psalmist promises that:

He that goeth forth and weepeth, bearing precious seed, shall doubtless *come again with rejoicing, bringing his sheaves with him.*

My previous impression of this passage was that my witnessing would only merit God's approval and produce sheaves if I sowed the seed of the Word of God while carrying such a heavy burden for lost souls, that I was to the point of tears. This thought had often troubled me, because I was not conscious of being burdened to the point of tears, so I had a guilt complex. I knew I didn't qualify in this area and could find no joy at the prospect of entering heaven with my arms full of sheaves that had been watered by my tears for souls. But now, through the message on the tape, I see that these tears could also be the result of being faithful in this area despite personal problems and difficulties that are known only to the Lord and me.

Another point that was cleared up that day was that the sheaves are not only a picture of people who are saved through our efforts in witnessing, but that sheaves can also be a result of our working for Him in other ways. The Holy Spirit produces the fruit of character in our lives, and this is often brought about through circumstances that cause tears. God rewards us for being faithful if we continue on sowing seed. Sheaves are also produced from seeds of love, joy, peace, long-suffering, gentleness, goodness, faith, meekness, and temperance. Since these seeds are only produced through the Spirit, they do not depend on my abilities, personality, or any human effort.

Recently I visited one of the dearest friends I have ever had. We have been friends for 38 years. This dear sister has had few opportunities to witness for the Lord because she is in a hospital bed in a private room. In spite of her sickness, that dear saint of God will carry bundles of sheaves to heaven with her that have been produced by the Holy Spirit. Hers has been an unbelievably hard life of physical and emotional pain, yet the Holy Spirit has been free to produce His sweet fruit within her. Her radiant face and her praise to the Lord gives witness to her inner rest and joy.

There will be great joy at the presentation of our sheaves to the Husbandman if we continue to go forth in our daily lives and sow the seed while we are weeping. In other words, if we don't stop what we are doing (even if all we are doing is lying in a hospital bed) simply because there are situations in life that cause tears and hopelessness, we will doubtless come again with rejoicing. Those very tears will have watered the fruit that matured into full-grown sheaves.

No matter what circumstances we face, it is always too early to quit sowing. Just ask God to keep your tears in His bottle (Ps. 56:8) They will bear testimony to our faithfulness and endurance. God promises that we will doubtless come again rejoicing, bringing our sheaves with us. He is a Man of His Word, so trust Him for this. He is the Corn of Wheat who died that He might not abide alone. And He deserves every sheaf we can bring Him.

28
THIRSTY? COME AND DRINK

"Beware that thou forget not the Lord thy God...who led thee through that great and terrible wilderness, wherein were fiery serpents, and scorpions, and drought, where there was no water; who brought thee forth water out of the rock of flint."
DEUTERONOMY 8:11, 15

Our two years in inland China were spent in an environment much like the setting in which Christ spoke the words recorded for us in John 7:37-38:

...Jesus stood and cried, saying, "If any man thirst, let him come unto Me, and drink. He that believeth on Me, as the scripture hath said, out of his heart shall flow rivers of living *water."*

An experience we had one day while there gave me an added appreciation for His invitation. I could well imagine the scene in which Jesus delivered these words: a hot, tiring day, with people milling all around Him. Since He was at an all-day Jewish festival, the Lord most likely was thirsty and realized that most of the people would be, too. We don't readily understand this kind of thirst today. We just go to a vending machine, a fast food or convenience store, or a public drinking fountain to quench our thirst. The people Jesus was addressing, however, knew real thirst. Their water had to be carried from public wells that were shared with hundreds of people. It was not easy to quench one's thirst immediately when it was felt.

We lived under conditions similar to those of Jesus' day, except that we didn't even have access to a public well! Our water was carried on the shoulders of a Chinese servant who had to get it from the river a good distance from our home. Every drop of water we used in our household was transported by buckets suspended from a bamboo pole on his shoulders. He emptied his buckets into large clay water pots that stood outside the kitchen door. We also had a drainage system through which rainwater was collected when it rained. One look into those water jars warned us not to drink from them directly—not ever!

Not only was the river a public water supply, it was the local laundromat and bathtub as well. The women beat their dirty clothes on stones and rinsed them in the river. Sewerage also drained into it. So every drop of water we consumed had to be thoroughly boiled.

Preparing drinking water was an important daily job for our cook boy. Our health depended on him. We had to trust his faithfulness in carrying out this procedure. The cook stove was a large, clay box-like arrangement in a shed a few yards away from the house, which protected the house from the smoke and fumes of an open charcoal fire. The cook boy had to boil the water, then set it aside to cool. Since we had no electricity, the coldest the water could become was room temperature.

One hot, summer day we had gone to distribute literature at a large public gathering. When we returned home late in the afternoon we were parched, to say the least. We wanted water to gulp down by the glassful, but when we reached for the water bottle, it was empty. We called the cook boy and asked him to bring us a drink. He soon appeared, red-faced, to apologize. He had forgotten that day to boil water, but assured us that he would soon boil some for tea.

Drinking tepid water was bad enough, but that day there was not even a drop of that! We were so thirsty it was even

144

tempting to get a drink from the clay water pots. The water didn't look all that bad—the polliwogs and dirt sort of stayed on the bottom, so the water on the top looked fairly clean. But to have drunk from the water pots would have been inviting trouble and, more likely, even death. To have to wait to drink hot tea stretched our patience, but we were grateful when he brought it to us a bit later. At a time like that, no price would have been too great to have paid for a glass of cold water fresh from an artesian well.

Christ might have had Jeremiah 2:13 in mind when He cried out His invitation:

For My people have committed two evils: they have forsaken Me, the fountain of living waters, and hewed out cisterns, broken cisterns, that can hold no water.

He used the term *living* waters. The water in the water pots that looked so inviting to us that hot day was the water of death. Cholera, dysentery, typhoid fever—you name it—were all around us. Any one of those could have been in our water pots. We had to wait for water that would sustain our lives, not threaten them. We were hot, tired, and dehydrated. It took self-control to wait for the boy to stir up the charcoal fire, boil the water, and make tea, but I might not be here today if we hadn't waited.

Surely Christ was not referring to physical water when He offered living water. He had something far greater in mind. The local wells could have supplied water for physical life with a little effort on their part. But Jesus knew that only He could supply the water for eternal life. Only He could satisfy their spiritual thirst.

Physical thirst is a God-given function of the human body when there is a rise in our salt level. The body craves water to help keep it healthy. We all know the serious problems that can result when we become dehydrated. If it were not for our thirst, we would forget to drink when we got too busy, and

145

would become sick. We drink because we are thirsty. We don't even think why we need to drink; we just drink and keep on drinking.

God also created us with the capacity for emotional and spiritual thirst. When our intake of spiritual water gets low, we feel a spiritual thirst. The unfortunate thing is, we seldom identify our spiritual thirst. Even when we do, our tendency is to immediately try to quench our thirst from the cisterns or clay water pots we have built for ourselves. We attribute our thirst to external causes such as circumstances and environment. We seldom are aware that our thirst is a thirst for God that occurs when we forget Him. When Christ stood to face the crowd at the feast, He offered to meet the thirst of everyone in the crowd, but few responded. When we ignore the source of *living water*, we invite in spiritual and emotional problems with various degrees of consequences.

Without doubt, Christ had salvation in mind when He extended His wonderful invitation to come to Him to quench our thirst, but I know that my spiritual and emotional thirsts were not all quenched as soon as I was born again. For years after that, I was still a very thirsty little girl. I was ten when I first took His invitation and came to Him and drank, but I still had many thirsts of discontentment. I couldn't wait to become a teenager so I could date. And when I became a teenager, I longed for marriage. After I married I thought that children would fill the void I still felt in my heart. I had children, but that still did not quench all my thirst by any means. I was never quite satisfied. There was always something more I longed for.

The Lord's complaint through Jeremiah was that His people began to forget Him and filled their lives in other ways. They built cisterns or clay water pots, which they drank from instead of going to the source of *living water*.

In our day, as in the days of Jeremiah, we forget that the diseases of sin are hiding in those cisterns. The water in our water pots in China had looked so inviting to us that hot day, but the germs were there. It was not pure water; it was terribly polluted. So it was with God's people and so it is with us.

I would be ashamed to tell you all the details, but I had been a missionary for years before the truth of Christ's full offer of living water became evident to me. I finally realized that our thirst is an ongoing thing. The deep longings I had, the feelings of loneliness, dissatisfaction, jealousy, worry, grumbling, and so on, were evidence that I was not sufficient in myself. They were God's reminders to me that I still needed to drink daily. It was then that I simply came to Him, just as I had for salvation so many years before, held out my cup to Him and said, "I'm thirsty, Lord, please give me a drink." The *living water* is found in the *living Word*.

Thirst is an ongoing need created by God to keep us constantly going to Christ for water. Instead of becoming discouraged by our thirst, we need to go more readily to Christ for His water. It's as simple as turning on a faucet. Just as I have to drink water to keep my physical body functioning properly, so I need to accept His invitation momentarily. He says, "Come and drink!"

29
WAITING

"Yea, let none that wait on Thee be ashamed: let them be ashamed which transgress without cause...Remember, O Lord, Thy tender mercies and Thy lovingkindnesses; for they have been ever of old."
PSALM 25:3, 6

One time I was asked what it really means to wait upon the Lord. I think the person who asked the question had Isaiah 40:31 in mind:

They that wait upon the Lord shall renew their strength; they shall mount up with wings as eagles; they shall run, and not be weary; and they shall walk, and not faint.

Scripture also tells us to wait for the Lord's return, but that instruction doesn't require an explanation. We've all waited for people and for events to start, and in the same way we simply have to wait for Him to come because we can do nothing else but wait. But how do we wait upon the Lord so that our strength is renewed as Isaiah promised? It's our attitude while waiting that determines our strength.

We all have spent hours waiting. Waiting in long lines. Waiting for people. Waiting for circumstances to develop. I distinctly remember one occasion when I'd been in line for a good, long time. As the line moved closer to the counter, it divided as one of several agents called us to the counter by turn. Just as I was in place to have been the next to be called, a lady appeared from nowhere and walked over to the agent in my place. I remember my feelings of injustice as she stepped ahead of me while I gathered my belongings. She did say, "Excuse me," but I was so put out by her rudeness that I didn't even answer her. I wasn't about to excuse her! This fact didn't seem to bother her at all. She went right on with her business and was out of there while I was still fuming. The delay was only a matter of five minutes, and I wasn't in that big a hurry, but I was put out because she infringed on my rights. We have our rights, don't we?

Why was I so disturbed at a five-minute delay? Why did her butting into the line upset me? I don't know, but I had been ignored as the agent attended to her, instead of sending her back and taking me first. It would have helped soothe my ruffled feathers if someone else had noticed the infringement, but no one mentioned the fact that I was next. Now, I don't like to be ignored. I and my business are pretty important to me and I think others should consider it so, too. Am I the only one who reacts like that? How about you?

As I've thought about waiting on the Lord and renewing our strength, this incident has come to mind again. I think that waiting on the Lord may be permitting Him to call someone else in line to be attended to, while I continue to wait. Waiting for a response to an unanswered prayer or blessing that I felt was far overdue are examples of ways in which we can wait upon the Lord. A five-minute delay is endurable, but if "my turn" is put off for months, or even years, I begin to fume and get out of sorts. When I get in that mood, I tire easily. I'm speaking from experience.

During one period, I felt that God was bypassing me, and answering the prayers of the other sisters in our senior Bible class prayer group. They were seeing marvelous answers to their prayers, and I was left standing in line. It was hard for me to see others attended to when I knew it was my turn. After all, I was a veteran Christian; they were still babes in Christ. My spiritual strength began to wane and I got extremely tired as I fumed. The thought actually passed through my mind, Why is God answering the prayers of these Japanese sisters before answering mine? Why are they seeing miracle-like answers and I'm seeing nothing spectacular? Frankly, under such circumstances, it was hard for me to "rejoice with those who do rejoice."

He's never too busy to care for my needs, but He often does have me wait for other people's convenience, for circumstances to unfold, or to develop my own maturity. God desires His children to grow up.

Whatever His reasons, I must accept His delays and wait patiently if I want Him to renew my strength. I am a servant and He is my Master. A servant who stands, patiently waiting for instructions, is often a better servant than the one who presumes to know what the Master wants, and goes ahead on her own without asking. It's a matter of acceptance without doubting the goodness of God that makes the difference.

Queen Esther is an example to me of what it means to wait on the Lord. Hers was an urgent emergency, yet she took three days to seek for strength and wisdom to do what she had to do. She waited until all the circumstances came together. She wasn't in a hurry to make her request to the king. She planned banquets and worked the details out in her mind beforehand. She worked hard while waiting. God honored her attitude of trust. Her peace of mind enabled her to think clearly and to place her life on the line. It gave her courage and strength to face the king.

When I remember in full confidence that God is working behind the scenes to accomplish His great, overall plan, it takes the stress and pressure out of waiting. In going to the eleventh chapter of Hebrews, we are reminded that some of God's faithful servants waited and waited, yet never saw deliverance in this life. Some saw miracles, others saw God's promises to them fulfilled in their lifetime, but some of them did not. Verse 39 offers a tremendously encouraging comment about those who did not:

And all these, having obtained a good report through faith, received not the promise.

As I see it, these saints had an inner witness that what God didn't do for them in this life He would fulfill in eternity. In either case, those whose promises were brought to fruition in this life, as well as those whose promises were not fulfilled here, found their faith to be sufficient to accept God's sovereignty. They were sustained in the midst of their waiting because they sensed the close link between life on earth and that in heaven. Therefore, they did not lose faith. They did not stumble when God did not perform what they thought He would, because they knew that God had not yet finished what He had promised. In faith they knew that He would be faithful to His Word.

The joy of knowing one is in the right place at the right time gives strength. The joy of the Lord gives the strength to keep on walking and not faint, to run without getting weary (Isa. 40:31) and then our wings will be strong enough to mount up, to be carried in His current, and to soar above the circumstances and difficulties of life.

30
WHAT IS MATURITY?

"And I said, This is my infirmity: but I will remember the years of the right hand of the most High...Thou hast with Thine arm redeemed Thy people...Selah."
PSALM 77:10, 15

Physical maturity is easy to recognize and requires very little explanation. Very few of us have any trouble maturing physically. If we eat and sleep properly, and are kept from sickness, it usually comes quite naturally. Emotional maturity is a bit harder to define, but it also is not difficult to recognize. Sadly enough, emotional immaturity is a lot more prevalent than physical immaturity.

Spiritual immaturity is far more common even than emotional immaturity. Often it is almost impossible to differentiate between emotional and spiritual immaturity because they are interrelated to some degree. I think emotional maturity equips us for personal relationships to those around us. Spiritual maturity is primarily toward God, but obviously affects our relationship with others, too.

One day as I puzzled over a friend of mine, I wondered why he had such trouble with his relationships with people. He is a very godly man. He knows his Scriptures and is without question a spiritually mature man. I thought, How can he be so filled with the Holy Spirit, and be so spiritually mature, and yet so immature emotionally? Then 1 Thessalonians 5:23 flashed into my mind:

And the very God of peace sanctify you wholly: and I pray God your whole spirit and soul and body be preserved blameless unto the coming of our Lord Jesus Christ.

It came to my attention that Paul prayed for maturity in all three areas—spirit, soul, and body. Evidently our service for the Lord will be hampered unless we mature in all areas. If, for one reason or another, growth has been hindered in any of these areas, there will be problems. Paul knew this, too, and prayed that the believers would mature in all three areas and so be kept blameless (not sinless) by facing, and dealing with, problems in their lives—a clear indication of maturity.

Using the physical realm as our guide, we can learn quite a bit about maturity. Although a child has been properly nourished and gets plenty of sleep, if his body is invaded by certain diseases, his growth will be affected. In the physical realm, the immune system takes over and counteracts this process naturally, but in the case of the other two realms, this is not so. It takes a conscious effort to rid the soul and spirit from similar invasions of hatred, lust, suspicion, and other forms of self-centeredness. Paul touches on this thought

Let us cleanse ourselves from all filthiness of the flesh and spirit, perfecting holiness in the fear of God (2 Cor. 7:1).

Since most of us reading this will have matured physically, let's concentrate on emotional and spiritual maturity. What is maturity? How can we measure maturity? How can we continue to mature?

Peter brings our thoughts to the need for milk in 1 Peter 2:2, "As newborn babes, desire the pure milk of the word, that ye may grow by it." The author of Hebrews (5:14) then brings us to the need of more solid foods.

But solid food belongeth to them that are of full age, even those who by reason of use have their senses exercised to discern both good and evil.

154

The author of Hebrews, in chapters 3 and 4, also brings our attention to the need for rest, which is another very important part of maturing. If we want to be healthy adult Christians, we must cease from our own efforts and trust God. We must enjoy the righteousness we have in Christ Jesus. Proper food and rest are important parts in our maturation, but the third point we come to, is also necessary.

The solid food of the Word of God is to give us the discernment we need, one of the signs of maturity. If ever we needed discernment, it is today. We need to be always growing in discernment to avoid the poisons that invade our thoughts. We also need to be discerning in the wise use of our time. It is so easy to let good things take the place of God's best.

While we were living in Japan, hundreds of Japanese volunteers lined up outside the Emperor's gate each day to clean the palace for him. It was an honor to work for the Emperor and his wife, even for one day. This has been a long-standing example to me. If they would work for their Emperor, surely I should count it a greater privilege to work for the King of kings and Lord of lords.

Maturity also brings discernment in our choice of materials from which to build our daily lives. Paul explains in 1 Corinthians 3:9-16 that some of the building materials will go up in smoke at the judgment seat of Christ. Other materials will endure the fire of His judgment. The gems that have been laid in the foundation on which we build will remain when the ashes from the temporal materials we used are blown away.

Another sign of maturity is patience. A mother who does not teach her child to learn to wait with the rest of the family, is doing an injustice. When a baby sees the bottle, it is quite normal for him to want it immediately (if not sooner). No child should expect this service after a few years. This truth was brought to me one day when a seven-year-old asked his mother why his baby sister was permitted to drink her milk before we prayed and he wasn't. She said to him, "You are a big boy now, and have to learn to wait. Your sister is just a baby."

Productivity is another evidence of maturity. Bearing fruit, whether in body or in the Holy Spirit, is a sure proof of developmental progress. The fruit of the Spirit yields recognizable fruit in our lives. Paul gave us a list of the most common fruit that should be seen in the life of every mature Christian (Gal. 5:22-23). I'm afraid that we often covet some of this fruit more than others, but they are all a sign of adult behavior. For instance, it is not surprising to see a baby entertaining a group with his or her antics as long as we ignore the mess, but at the end of the meal when the washcloth comes out—well, that is a different story! Maturity brings awareness of our need for constant cleansing of our attitudes if we are to be acceptable in adult society. Self-control gives the ability to accept the washcloth of cleansing if other Christians feel we need it.

Well mannered, well behaved, mature, believers are monuments to God's grace and a credit to Him. Let's become those whom He will be happy to acknowledge as His children.

31
WIN BY LOSING

"But call to remembrance the former days, in which, after ye were illuminated, ye endured a great fight of afflictions; partly, whilst ye were made a gazingstock both by reproaches and afflictions; and partly, whilst ye became companions of them that were so used. For ye had compassion of me in my bonds, and took joyfully the spoiling of your goods, knowing in yourselves that ye have in heaven a better and an enduring substance. Cast not away therefore your confidence, which hath great recompence of reward."
HEBREWS 10:32-35

On the night of the big banquet to welcome me back to Japan in 1992, a white-haired gentleman gave his testimony concerning the grace of God in his life. Although he had prematurely white hair, his face was still the face of a young man, his body was of small stature and extremely dignified. His big smile and friendly manner supported all he was saying. However, my mind was not wanting to follow the message he was giving, because early in his message the position of the table at which we were sitting struck me. They had arranged that the guest table stood as nearly as possible over the spot where our dining room table had stood, before the old house had been bulldozed down to make room for the lovely new chapel.

The memory of the old table kept coming back, and I could not push it away. I saw again the students sitting around after dinner, with songbooks and Bibles on the table. There had always been singing, Bible reading, and lots of questions asked. As a college freshman, night after night, he sat with the others. The emphasis in the Bible class at the college was largely gospel, but at the dinner table, more basic truths of the Scriptures were taught because these students had a special interest and a desire to learn. After his salvation, it was there that he was taught the foundational principles of the church. He never seemed to tire of talking about the Lord Jesus Christ. Week after week he came home with Gifford to have dinner with us, so that he could accompany Gifford to a cottage meeting in the evening. The others would go to the evening meeting occasionally, but he seldom missed.

I hope I looked interested in what he was saying, but in my mind I was tracing his story from his conversion to the place where he stood that evening, thirty years later. I marveled again that God should have reached down into the very heart of Japan, into a small country town, and sent this young man to the city of Takasaki for his education. It was amazing to me that the Lord should have opened the door for Bible classes in the college he attended. From the first time Gifford and he met, Gifford sensed his unusual searching for spiritual truths. After God saved him, he made rapid progress. The night he was saved is a story in itself. It was Ruth's birthday and we had to wait for Gifford to have our cake.

After graduation, he miraculously was offered a position in a silk factory. Because of his keen mind and ability to take responsibility, he soon worked his way up in the company. Within a very few years the president of the company died suddenly, opening a place for him in the administration. It is almost unheard of in Japan for a man that young to be in such an important place of responsibility. Family, friends, and church members were delighted for him. No one ever entertained the thought that he might not accept the offer. Everyone assumed that he would grab the opportunity.

Instead, it unleashed a bitter struggle within him. Half of

his heart reasoned that the Lord would be glorified through this quick rise to power. He was married and could well use the added finances for their family, and have plenty to help in the work of the Lord. He was tempted to reason that he could serve the Lord much better as a prestigious, successful businessman. But at the same time, deep down in the recess of his own heart, he became aware that God had something far better in mind for him. He didn't want to disappoint his Lord.

The battle that followed would fill a book, but I'll share a few of the highlights. He knew the pitfalls that could be hidden in the future. Having been in the company for several years, he knew that most of the company policies were made on weekend trips to various hot springs in the mountains. Being away from his family for the weekend offered temptations of their own making. He also knew that with the added responsibility came longer hours that would encroach on the regular church services, especially on Sundays. To him, the Lord's Day was the highlight of the week, and he could not bear to use it for anything else.

When he mentioned all these factors to his wife, she shared his misgivings. His next step was to share both sides of the problem with Gifford. The two of them spent hours together, praying for the Lord's guidance. They evaluated the list of advantages to see if, in the light of the Bible, they would be worth the spiritual losses.

The real blow came when he decided not to take the position. When he informed the administration why, they bluntly told him that if he didn't accept their offer, he would have to leave the company. This meant starting all over again in his business career, which proved to be a far greater battle than any of us had imagined. The opposition from both families, being out of work, along with the misunderstanding of friends, made it even harder to follow through with what he felt the Lord was guiding him to do.

It seemed many times during that first year or two that God

159

had indeed let him down, and had not honored his decision. However, through the faithful support of his dear wife, this test of faith did not stumble him. Rather, it strengthened their faith together. After two or three temporary jobs, the Lord led a Christian employer to offer him a position of leadership in his company.

Fortunately, when I reached that stage in my private wanderings, I became aware that he had concluded his message. But as I watched his face, and noticed the openness with which he spoke, and saw the sparkle in his eyes, I knew that he held no regrets for the sacrifice he had made for Christ and His church. The clearness of his speech and the power of his message were evidence to me that his choice had been the right one.

Later in the week, I had the joy of holding their first grandchild and visited with the wife's mother, who is now a radiant Christian. I also visited the company of his present employment, and sensed his joy and gratitude as he ushered me into his private office. The smile as he sat behind the large desk, which seemed to swallow him up, gave proof that God's will for his life was really good. It was perfect, and it certainly was acceptable to all of us now. The Lord has once more opened up a responsible position for him in a thriving business. He has significant free time to give to the Lord. He is asked to minister in various assemblies in the area. His life stands as a witness to the goodness of God. God is using him to encourage many others who are facing difficult decisions. Their stand has helped others to stand uncompromisingly for the Lord. He is living proof of the divine challenge: *"Them that honor Me, I will honor."*